Edward D. Andrews

IS THE BIBLE REALLY THE WORD OF GOD?

Is Christianity the One True Faith?

IS THE BIBLE REALLY THE WORD OF GOD?

Is Christianity the One True Faith?

Edward D. Andrews

Christian Publishing House
Cambridge, Ohio

Copyright © 2017, 2024 Edward D. Andrews

All rights reserved. Except for brief quotations in articles, other publications, book reviews, and blogs, no part of this book may be reproduced in any manner without prior written permission from the publishers. For information, write, support@christianpublishers.org

IS THE BIBLE REALLY THE WORD OF GOD? Is Christianity the One True Faith? by Edward D. Andrews

ISBN-13: 978-1-945757-46-4

ISBN-10: 1-945757-46-9

Table of Contents

Preface 7

Introduction 9

SECTION 1 THE BATTLE FOR HE BIBLE 11

CHAPTER 1 Why Should We Consider the Bible? 12

CHAPTER 2 How Can We Know the Bible Is True? 17

CHAPTER 3 Just How Much Does Archaeology Support the Bible? 22

CHAPTER 4 How Reliable Is the Old Testament? 27

CHAPTER 5 How Reliable Is the New Testament? 33

CHAPTER 6 Did the Miracles Really Happen? 38

CHAPTER 7 Did Jesus Really Exist? 44

CHAPTER 8 The Resurrection of Jesus, Did It Really Happen? 49

CHAPTER 9 What about the Mistakes, Errors, And Contradictions in the Bible? 54

CHAPTER 10 Has Science Proved the Bible Wrong? 60

CHAPTER 11 How Can We Know That Any of the Prophecies Come True? 67

CHAPTER 12 How Can We Explain So Many Bible Difficulties? 73

CHAPTER 13 How Can We Know the Bible Is Authentic and True? 115

CHAPTER 14 How is the Bible Is Practical for Our Day?. 123

CHAPTER 15 Infallibility and Absolute Inerrancy of Scripture, Really? 129

CHAPTER 16 Is the Word of God Really Alive? 134

CHAPTER 17 How Does the Bible Relate to You? 141

SECTION 2 EMBATTLED CHRISTIANITY 148

CHAPTER 18 Christianity—Was Jesus the Way to God? .. 149

CHAPTER 19 Why Are There So Many Christian Denominations?... 157

CHAPTER 20 The Great Apostasy—The Way to God Blocked in the Middle Ages 164

CHAPTER 21 The Reformation—The Search for God...... 170

CHAPTER 22 Modern Disbelief—Liberal to Moderate Christianity... 177

CHAPTER 23 The Battle for the Bible— A Return to the True God.. 182

Preface

In a world increasingly skeptical of religious claims and ancient texts, the Bible stands at the center of intense debate. Questions about its authenticity, historical reliability, and theological soundness are not new, but they are more pressing than ever in our modern, scientifically-oriented society. As believers, it is imperative to address these questions with clarity, conviction, and a robust understanding of the evidence that supports our faith.

This book, **Is the Bible Really the Word of God? Is Christianity the One True Faith?**, is born out of a deep passion for defending the truth of the Scriptures and the core tenets of Christianity. Over the years, I have encountered numerous individuals, both believers and skeptics, who grapple with these profound questions. Their inquiries have driven me to delve deeper into the historical, archaeological, and textual evidence that underpins the Bible's claims. It is my hope that this book will serve as a comprehensive resource for those seeking to understand and defend the Christian faith.

The first section of this book, "The Battle for the Bible," addresses the myriad challenges posed by modern scholarship, scientific discoveries, and common misconceptions. It begins by exploring why we should consider the Bible, moving through detailed discussions on its truthfulness, archaeological support, and the reliability of both the Old and New Testaments. We will also examine the reality of miracles, the historical existence of Jesus, and the evidence for His resurrection. Each chapter is designed to equip you with the knowledge and confidence to stand firm in your faith.

The second section, "Embattled Christianity," delves into the historical and doctrinal struggles faced by the church. From the early schisms and the Great Apostasy to the Reformation and the rise of modern disbelief, this section traces the challenges and victories that have shaped Christian doctrine and practice. By understanding these historical contexts, we gain insight into the ongoing battle for the Bible and the need for a return to the true God.

This book is not just an academic exercise; it is a call to action. It is a call for believers to reaffirm their commitment to the authority of Scripture and the truth of the Gospel. It is a call to engage thoughtfully and respectfully with skeptics, providing reasoned answers to their questions. Most importantly, it is a call to live out the transformative power of God's Word in our daily lives.

I invite you to embark on this journey with an open heart and a discerning mind. As you read, may you be strengthened in your faith and equipped to defend the truth of the Bible and the Christian faith.

Edward D. Andrews

Author of 220+ books

Introduction

The Bible, an ancient collection of texts spanning centuries, cultures, and continents, has been revered by billions as the divinely inspired Word of God. Its pages have guided countless individuals in their spiritual journeys, offering wisdom, comfort, and instruction. Yet, in our contemporary world, the Bible faces relentless scrutiny and skepticism. Questions about its authenticity, historical accuracy, and relevance abound, challenging believers to defend their faith with reason and evidence.

The aim of this book is to address these questions head-on, providing a comprehensive defense of the Bible and the Christian faith. We live in an age where information is abundant, but so is misinformation. Popular media, academic circles, and even some religious institutions often present views that undermine the traditional understanding of Scripture. This book seeks to cut through the noise, presenting a clear, reasoned case for why the Bible is indeed the Word of God and why Christianity stands as the true faith.

This exploration is divided into two main sections. The first, "The Battle for the Bible," delves into the evidence supporting the Bible's reliability and divine inspiration. We will examine archaeological findings that corroborate biblical narratives, the consistency and preservation of biblical texts, and the fulfillment of prophecies that point to a divine hand in history. Additionally, we will tackle challenging questions about apparent contradictions, scientific criticisms, and the miracles recorded in Scripture.

The second section, "Embattled Christianity," traces the historical and doctrinal challenges the church has faced from its inception to the present day. From early heresies and schisms to the profound impact of the Reformation and the rise of modern liberal theology, this section offers an in-depth look at how Christianity has defended its core truths against various attacks. Understanding this history is crucial, as it equips us to recognize and respond to contemporary challenges with the same vigor and conviction.

Throughout this journey, our approach is rooted in the conservative evangelical tradition, emphasizing the historical-grammatical method of interpretation. This method respects the text's original context and intended meaning, avoiding the pitfalls of modern critical methods that often undermine the Bible's authority. By adhering to this approach, we aim to present a faithful and compelling case for the Bible's divine origin and the truth of Christianity.

As we embark on this exploration, it is essential to approach these topics with both intellectual rigor and spiritual humility. The goal is not merely to win arguments but to deepen our understanding and strengthen our faith. Whether you are a believer seeking to bolster your convictions or a skeptic searching for answers, this book invites you to engage thoughtfully with the evidence and consider the profound implications of the Bible's message.

May this journey enrich your understanding and inspire a deeper appreciation for the enduring truth of God's Word.

SECTION 1 THE BATTLE FOR HE BIBLE

Edward D. Andrews

CHAPTER 1 Why Should We Consider the Bible?

The Divine Inspiration of Scripture

The Bible's divine inspiration is foundational to understanding its reliability and trustworthiness. According to 2 Timothy 3:16, "All Scripture is inspired by God and beneficial for teaching, for reproof, for correction, for training in righteousness." This passage underscores the belief that the Bible is not merely a human creation but is breathed out by God Himself. This divine origin means that the Scriptures carry the authority of God and are therefore completely trustworthy.

The process of inspiration ensures that the Bible's authors, while employing their unique styles and perspectives, conveyed God's message without error. As stated in 2 Peter 1:21, "For no prophecy was ever made by an act of human will, but men moved by the Holy Spirit spoke from God." This verse highlights the role of the Holy Spirit in guiding the biblical authors, ensuring the accuracy and divine authority of their writings.

Historical and Archaeological Evidence

The historical reliability of the Bible is corroborated by numerous archaeological findings. One significant example is the discovery of the Dead Sea Scrolls in 1947. These ancient manuscripts include portions of the Hebrew Bible and have demonstrated the remarkable consistency of the biblical text over centuries. The Isaiah Scroll, for instance, dates back to the 2nd century B.C.E. and aligns closely with the Masoretic Text of Isaiah used today.

Moreover, archaeological excavations have unearthed evidence supporting the existence of biblical figures and events. The Tel Dan Stele, discovered in northern Israel, contains an inscription referring to the "House of David," providing tangible evidence for the historical King David mentioned in 1 Samuel 16:13. Similarly, the Moabite Stone

IS THE BIBLE REALLY THE WORD OF GOD?

(Mesha Stele) references the Israelite king Omri, mentioned in 1 Kings 16:23-28, confirming the biblical account's historical accuracy.

Prophetic Fulfillment

The fulfillment of biblical prophecies serves as compelling evidence for the Bible's divine inspiration and reliability. Isaiah 53, written around 700 B.C.E., vividly describes the suffering and atoning death of the Messiah, which Christians believe was fulfilled in Jesus Christ. Isaiah 53:5 states, "But he was pierced through for our transgressions, he was crushed for our iniquities; the chastening for our well-being fell upon him, and by his scourging we are healed." This prophecy's precise fulfillment in the life and crucifixion of Jesus, as recorded in the New Testament, underscores the Bible's prophetic reliability.

Additionally, the prophecies concerning the rise and fall of empires, such as those found in Daniel 2 and 7, have been historically validated. Daniel 2:44, for example, predicts the establishment of an eternal kingdom by God, which Christians interpret as the Kingdom of God inaugurated by Jesus. These fulfilled prophecies demonstrate the Bible's accuracy and divine foreknowledge, further establishing its trustworthiness.

Manuscript Evidence and Textual Reliability

The Bible's textual reliability is supported by the abundance and quality of its manuscript evidence. The New Testament, in particular, boasts an unparalleled number of ancient manuscripts, with over 5,800 Greek manuscripts, 10,000 Latin manuscripts, and thousands more in various languages. This wealth of manuscripts allows scholars to reconstruct the original text with a high degree of confidence.

One notable manuscript is the Codex Sinaiticus, dating to the 4th century C.E., which contains the entire New Testament. The consistency of these early manuscripts with later copies underscores the careful transmission of the biblical text over the centuries. Moreover, textual criticism, the scholarly practice of comparing these manuscripts, has confirmed that the variations among them are minor and do not affect core Christian doctrines.

Internal Consistency and Unity

The Bible's internal consistency and unity, despite being written over 1,500 years by more than 40 authors from diverse backgrounds, is remarkable. This unity is evident in the coherent narrative and consistent themes that run throughout the Scriptures. From Genesis to Revelation, the Bible tells a unified story of God's creation, human fall, redemption, and the ultimate restoration of all things.

This consistency is particularly evident in the fulfillment of Old Testament prophecies in the New Testament. For instance, Micah 5:2 predicts the Messiah's birth in Bethlehem, which is fulfilled in Matthew 2:1. This seamless integration of prophecy and fulfillment across different books and authors points to a divine orchestration beyond human capability, affirming the Bible's reliability.

The Bible's Transformative Power

The transformative power of the Bible in individuals' lives and societies provides experiential evidence of its divine origin and trustworthiness. Hebrews 4:12 states, "For the word of God is living and active and sharper than any two-edged sword, and piercing as far as the division of soul and spirit, of both joints and marrow, and able to judge the thoughts and intentions of the heart." This verse highlights the Bible's unique ability to convict, guide, and transform hearts and minds.

Throughout history, countless individuals have testified to the life-changing impact of reading and applying the Bible. From the early church fathers to modern-day believers, the Bible has inspired faith, moral transformation, and a deeper relationship with God. The societal impact of the Bible is also evident in the establishment of hospitals, schools, and charitable organizations motivated by biblical principles.

The Role of Faith and Reason

While historical, archaeological, and manuscript evidence provide strong support for the Bible's reliability, faith also plays a crucial role in accepting its divine authority. Hebrews 11:1 defines faith as "the assurance of things hoped for, the conviction of things not seen." This assurance is not blind belief but is based on the reasonable evidence and the internal witness of the Holy Spirit.

Christian apologetics bridges the gap between faith and reason, demonstrating that believing in the Bible is intellectually viable and spiritually enriching. As 1 Peter 3:15 exhorts, "But sanctify Christ as Lord in your hearts, always being ready to make a defense to everyone who asks you to give an account for the hope that is in you, yet with gentleness and reverence." This call to defend the faith underscores the importance of understanding and articulating the reasons for trusting the Bible.

Addressing Common Objections

Common objections to the Bible's reliability often stem from misunderstandings or misinterpretations of the text. For example, some critics argue that the presence of miracles in the Bible undermines its credibility. However, miracles, by definition, are extraordinary events that signify divine intervention. The resurrection of Jesus, a central miracle in Christianity, is supported by historical evidence and eyewitness testimonies, as recorded in 1 Corinthians 15:3-8.

Another objection concerns the perceived contradictions in the Bible. A careful study using the Historical-Grammatical method of interpretation reveals that these apparent contradictions often result from a lack of understanding of the cultural, historical, and linguistic context. When properly interpreted, the Bible's messages are coherent and consistent, reinforcing its reliability.

The Importance of a Literal Interpretation

A literal interpretation of the Bible, using the Historical-Grammatical method, ensures that the text is understood as intended by its original authors. This approach respects the genre, historical context, and grammatical structure of the biblical writings, avoiding the pitfalls of subjective interpretations. As stated in Nehemiah 8:8, "They read from the book, from the law of God, translating to give the sense so that they understood the reading." This approach seeks to uncover the original meaning and apply it faithfully to contemporary contexts.

Literal Bible chronology, for example, provides a clear framework for understanding the timeline of biblical events. By adhering to the literal dates given in Scripture, such as the creation of the world around 4,000 B.C.E. and the Exodus around 1446 B.C.E., believers can align historical events with biblical narratives, enhancing the coherence and reliability of the Bible.

Conclusion on Considering the Bible

The reliability and trustworthiness of the Bible are grounded in its divine inspiration, historical and archaeological evidence, prophetic fulfillment, manuscript evidence, internal consistency, and transformative power. A careful and literal interpretation of the Scriptures, supported by faith and reason, allows believers to confidently trust the Bible as the authoritative Word of God. By addressing common objections and understanding the importance of the Historical-Grammatical method, Christians can robustly defend their faith and encourage others to consider the Bible's profound truths.

CHAPTER 2 How Can We Know the Bible Is True?

The Foundation of Divine Inspiration

The bedrock of the Bible's trustworthiness lies in its divine inspiration. As stated in 2 Timothy 3:16, "All Scripture is inspired by God and beneficial for teaching, for reproof, for correction, for training in righteousness." This passage asserts that the Bible is not a product of human intellect but is breathed out by God Himself, ensuring that the Scriptures are divinely authoritative and completely trustworthy.

This process of inspiration is further explained in 2 Peter 1:21: "For no prophecy was ever made by an act of human will, but men moved by the Holy Spirit spoke from God." This highlights the divine guidance that the biblical authors received, ensuring that what they wrote was free from error and precisely what God intended to communicate. Understanding that the Bible is divinely inspired reassures us of its absolute reliability and accuracy.

Historical and Archaeological Corroboration

The Bible's historical reliability is substantiated by numerous archaeological findings. One of the most significant discoveries is the Dead Sea Scrolls, found in 1947. These ancient manuscripts, which include portions of nearly every book of the Hebrew Bible, have demonstrated the remarkable consistency of the biblical text over centuries. The Isaiah Scroll, dating back to the 2nd century B.C.E., matches closely with the Masoretic Text of Isaiah used today, confirming the faithful transmission of the Scriptures.

Archaeological excavations have also unearthed evidence supporting the existence of biblical figures and events. For instance, the Tel Dan Stele, discovered in northern Israel, contains an inscription referring to the "House of David," providing tangible evidence for the historical King David mentioned in 1 Samuel 16:13.

Similarly, the Moabite Stone (Mesha Stele) references the Israelite king Omri, mentioned in 1 Kings 16:23-28, confirming the Bible's historical accounts.

Prophecies Fulfilled in Detail

The fulfillment of biblical prophecies serves as compelling evidence of the Bible's divine inspiration and reliability. For example, Isaiah 53, written around 700 B.C.E., vividly describes the suffering and atoning death of the Messiah, which Christians believe was fulfilled in Jesus Christ. Isaiah 53:5 states, "But he was pierced through for our transgressions, he was crushed for our iniquities; the chastening for our well-being fell upon him, and by his scourging we are healed." The precise fulfillment of this prophecy in the life and crucifixion of Jesus, as recorded in the New Testament, underscores the Bible's prophetic accuracy.

Moreover, the prophecies concerning the rise and fall of empires, such as those found in Daniel 2 and 7, have been historically validated. Daniel 2:44 predicts the establishment of an eternal kingdom by God, which Christians interpret as the Kingdom of God inaugurated by Jesus. These fulfilled prophecies demonstrate the Bible's divine foreknowledge and further establish its reliability.

Manuscript Evidence and Textual Integrity

The textual reliability of the Bible is supported by the abundance and quality of its manuscript evidence. The New Testament, in particular, boasts an unparalleled number of ancient manuscripts, with over 5,800 Greek manuscripts, 10,000 Latin manuscripts, and thousands more in various languages. This wealth of manuscripts allows scholars to reconstruct the original text with a high degree of confidence.

One notable manuscript is the Codex Sinaiticus, dating to the 4th century C.E., which contains the entire New Testament. The consistency of these early manuscripts with later copies underscores the careful transmission of the biblical text over the centuries. Textual criticism, the scholarly practice of comparing these manuscripts, has confirmed that the variations among them are minor and do not affect core Christian doctrines.

IS THE BIBLE REALLY THE WORD OF GOD?

Internal Consistency and Coherence

The Bible's internal consistency and coherence, despite being written over 1,500 years by more than 40 authors from diverse backgrounds, is remarkable. This unity is evident in the coherent narrative and consistent themes that run throughout the Scriptures. From Genesis to Revelation, the Bible tells a unified story of God's creation, human fall, redemption, and the ultimate restoration of all things.

This consistency is particularly evident in the fulfillment of Old Testament prophecies in the New Testament. For example, Micah 5:2 predicts the Messiah's birth in Bethlehem, which is fulfilled in Matthew 2:1. This seamless integration of prophecy and fulfillment across different books and authors points to a divine orchestration beyond human capability, affirming the Bible's reliability.

The Transformative Power of the Bible

The transformative power of the Bible in individuals' lives and societies provides experiential evidence of its divine origin and trustworthiness. Hebrews 4:12 states, "For the word of God is living and active and sharper than any two-edged sword, and piercing as far as the division of soul and spirit, of both joints and marrow, and able to judge the thoughts and intentions of the heart." This verse highlights the Bible's unique ability to convict, guide, and transform hearts and minds.

Throughout history, countless individuals have testified to the life-changing impact of reading and applying the Bible. From the early church fathers to modern-day believers, the Bible has inspired faith, moral transformation, and a deeper relationship with God. The societal impact of the Bible is also evident in the establishment of hospitals, schools, and charitable organizations motivated by biblical principles.

Faith and Reason in Harmony

While historical, archaeological, and manuscript evidence provide strong support for the Bible's reliability, faith also plays a crucial role in accepting its divine authority. Hebrews 11:1 defines faith as "the assurance of things hoped for, the conviction of things not seen." This assurance is not blind belief but is based on reasonable evidence and the internal witness of the Holy Spirit.

Christian apologetics bridges the gap between faith and reason, demonstrating that believing in the Bible is intellectually viable and spiritually enriching. As 1 Peter 3:15 exhorts, "But sanctify Christ as Lord in your hearts, always being ready to make a defense to everyone who asks you to give an account for the hope that is in you, yet with gentleness and reverence." This call to defend the faith underscores the importance of understanding and articulating the reasons for trusting the Bible.

Addressing Common Objections

Common objections to the Bible's reliability often stem from misunderstandings or misinterpretations of the text. For example, some critics argue that the presence of miracles in the Bible undermines its credibility. However, miracles, by definition, are extraordinary events that signify divine intervention. The resurrection of Jesus, a central miracle in Christianity, is supported by historical evidence and eyewitness testimonies, as recorded in 1 Corinthians 15:3-8.

Another objection concerns the perceived contradictions in the Bible. A careful study using the Historical-Grammatical method of interpretation reveals that these apparent contradictions often result from a lack of understanding of the cultural, historical, and linguistic context. When properly interpreted, the Bible's messages are coherent and consistent, reinforcing its reliability.

Literal Interpretation and Historical-Grammatical Method

A literal interpretation of the Bible, using the Historical-Grammatical method, ensures that the text is understood as intended by its original authors. This approach respects the genre, historical context, and grammatical structure of the biblical writings, avoiding the pitfalls of subjective interpretations. As stated in Nehemiah 8:8, "They read from the book, from the law of God, translating to give the sense so that they understood the reading." This approach seeks to uncover the original meaning and apply it faithfully to contemporary contexts.

Literal Bible chronology, for example, provides a clear framework for understanding the timeline of biblical events. By adhering to the literal dates given in Scripture, such as the creation of the world around 4,000 B.C.E. and the Exodus around 1446 B.C.E., believers can align historical events with biblical narratives, enhancing the coherence and reliability of the Bible.

The Role of the Spirit-Inspired Word of God

It is essential to understand that Christians are guided by the Spirit-inspired Word of God rather than an indwelling of the Holy Spirit. As John 16:13 applies only to the apostles, we rely on the Bible for guidance and understanding. The Scriptures provide the necessary wisdom and instruction for living a life pleasing to God. Psalm 119:105 states, "Your word is a lamp to my feet and a light to my path," highlighting the Bible's role in guiding believers.

The Bible's Enduring Relevance

The Bible's relevance extends beyond its historical and prophetic accuracy. It addresses fundamental human questions and provides moral and spiritual guidance that transcends time and culture. The teachings of Jesus, such as the Sermon on the Mount in Matthew 5-7, offer timeless principles for ethical living and interpersonal relationships. The Bible's enduring relevance is a testament to its divine origin and the truth it conveys.

The Testimony of Jesus

Jesus Christ Himself affirmed the trustworthiness of the Scriptures. In Matthew 5:18, He stated, "For truly I say to you, until heaven and earth pass away, not the smallest letter or stroke shall pass from the Law until all is accomplished." Jesus' affirmation of the Scriptures underscores their divine authority and reliability. His fulfillment of Old Testament prophecies and His teachings further validate the truth of the Bible.

Edward D. Andrews

CHAPTER 3 Just How Much Does Archaeology Support the Bible?

The Role of Archaeology in Biblical Validation

Archaeology plays a significant role in validating the historical reliability of the Bible. Over the past 150 years, thousands of discoveries have corroborated the biblical narrative, affirming its accuracy and trustworthiness. The study of ancient artifacts, inscriptions, and structures has provided tangible evidence that supports the events, people, and places described in the Scriptures. This field of study serves as an important tool for understanding and confirming the biblical text.

Discoveries Supporting the Patriarchal Narratives

The accounts of the patriarchs—Abraham, Isaac, Jacob, and Joseph—form the foundation of Israel's history. Archaeological findings have provided substantial support for these narratives. For example, the discovery of the Nuzi Tablets, which date back to the 15th century B.C.E., reveals customs and laws similar to those described in Genesis. These tablets confirm practices such as the adoption of heirs, the inheritance rights of women, and the significance of household gods, aligning with the stories of Abraham and Jacob (Genesis 15:2-4; Genesis 31:19).

The city of Ur, identified as Abraham's birthplace (Genesis 11:31), has been excavated, revealing a highly advanced civilization. The findings include ziggurats, royal tombs, and numerous artifacts that illustrate the wealth and culture of Ur during Abraham's time, around 2000 B.C.E. This evidence supports the biblical account of Abraham's departure from a prosperous and sophisticated city to follow Jehovah's call.

Corroboration of the Exodus and Conquest

IS THE BIBLE REALLY THE WORD OF GOD?

The Exodus is a pivotal event in Israel's history, and while direct evidence of the Israelites' presence in Egypt and their subsequent exodus is limited, several archaeological discoveries provide indirect support. The Brooklyn Papyrus, dating to around 1740 B.C.E., lists the names of slaves in Egypt, many of which are Semitic, indicating the presence of a significant Semitic population in Egypt during the period traditionally associated with the Israelites' enslavement.

The Merneptah Stele, dating to around 1208 B.C.E., contains the earliest extra-biblical reference to Israel, stating that "Israel is laid waste, his seed is not." This inscription confirms that a people known as Israel were present in Canaan during the late 13th century B.C.E., shortly after the traditional date of the Exodus around 1446 B.C.E.

Archaeological excavations at Jericho have revealed evidence of a city that was destroyed and subsequently abandoned during the late Bronze Age, which aligns with the biblical account of Joshua's conquest (Joshua 6:20-21). The discovery of collapsed walls and a layer of ash suggests a violent destruction, supporting the narrative of the walls falling after the Israelites' assault.

The United Monarchy: David and Solomon

The existence of King David and his dynasty has been a topic of debate among scholars. However, the discovery of the Tel Dan Stele in 1993 provided the first extra-biblical evidence of David's dynasty. The stele, dating to the 9th century B.C.E., contains an Aramaic inscription referring to the "House of David." This discovery confirms the biblical account of David's rule and his significance in Israel's history (1 Samuel 16:13; 2 Samuel 5:3-4).

Solomon's reign, described as a period of great prosperity and building projects, is also supported by archaeological findings. Excavations at Megiddo, Hazor, and Gezer have uncovered structures that match the description of Solomon's building activities in 1 Kings 9:15. These include gates and fortifications that reflect a centralized and powerful administration consistent with Solomon's kingdom.

Evidence from the Divided Kingdoms

The period of the divided kingdoms of Israel and Judah is well-documented archaeologically. The Mesha Stele, also known as the Moabite Stone, dates to the 9th century B.C.E. and recounts the rebellion of King Mesha of Moab against Israel, as described in 2 Kings 3:4-27. This stele corroborates the biblical account of the conflict between Moab and Israel, providing a valuable historical context.

The Lachish Reliefs, found in the palace of Sennacherib at Nineveh, depict the Assyrian siege and conquest of Lachish in 701 B.C.E., an event recorded in 2 Kings 18:13-14. These reliefs provide a detailed visual representation of the siege, confirming the biblical narrative of the Assyrian invasion during King Hezekiah's reign.

The Babylonian Exile and Return

The Babylonian exile, a significant event in Jewish history, is also supported by archaeological evidence. The Babylonian Chronicles, a series of clay tablets, describe the conquest of Jerusalem by Nebuchadnezzar II in 597 B.C.E., as recorded in 2 Kings 24:10-14. These tablets confirm the biblical account of the fall of Jerusalem and the deportation of its inhabitants to Babylon.

The Cyrus Cylinder, an ancient clay artifact, contains an edict from King Cyrus of Persia, allowing exiled peoples, including the Jews, to return to their homelands and rebuild their temples. This decree, issued in 539 B.C.E., aligns with the biblical account of Cyrus's proclamation in 2 Chronicles 36:22-23 and Ezra 1:1-4, confirming the historical accuracy of the Jewish return from exile.

New Testament Corroboration

The New Testament is also richly supported by archaeological discoveries. The existence of Pontius Pilate, the Roman governor who sentenced Jesus to crucifixion, is confirmed by the Pilate Stone, an inscription found in Caesarea Maritima. This stone, dating to the 1st century C.E., bears Pilate's name and title, corroborating the New Testament account (Matthew 27:2; John 19:1).

The Pool of Bethesda, mentioned in John 5:2 as the site where Jesus healed a paralytic, has been excavated in Jerusalem. The discovery of this pool, with its five porticoes, matches the description given in the Gospel of John, providing further evidence for the accuracy of the New Testament narratives.

The Reliability of Luke as a Historian

The Gospel of Luke and the Acts of the Apostles, both written by Luke, have been validated through numerous archaeological findings. Sir William Ramsay, a renowned archaeologist, initially doubted the historical accuracy of Luke's writings. However, after extensive research and excavations in Asia Minor, Ramsay concluded that Luke was a highly reliable historian. Luke's precise descriptions of geographical locations, political titles, and cultural practices have been consistently confirmed by archaeological evidence.

For example, in Acts 17:6-8, Luke refers to city officials in Thessalonica as "politarchs," a term not found in classical literature. Archaeological discoveries, including an inscription on an arch in Thessalonica, have since confirmed the use of this title in the first century C.E., affirming Luke's accuracy.

The Dead Sea Scrolls: A Testament to Textual Integrity

The Dead Sea Scrolls, discovered between 1947 and 1956 in the Qumran caves near the Dead Sea, are one of the most significant archaeological finds of the 20th century. These ancient manuscripts, which include portions of nearly every book of the Hebrew Bible, date back to the 3rd century B.C.E. to the 1st century C.E. The scrolls have provided invaluable insights into the textual transmission of the Hebrew Scriptures and confirmed the reliability of the Masoretic Text.

One of the most remarkable scrolls is the Great Isaiah Scroll, which dates to around 150 B.C.E. This scroll contains the entire book of Isaiah and aligns closely with the Masoretic Text, demonstrating the faithful preservation of the biblical text over centuries. The consistency between the Dead Sea Scrolls and later manuscripts attests to the meticulous care taken by scribes in copying the Scriptures.

Conclusion of Archaeological Support

Archaeological discoveries have consistently supported the historical reliability of the Bible. From the patriarchal narratives to the New Testament accounts, the findings of archaeologists have corroborated the events, people, and places described in the Scriptures. This body of evidence affirms that the Bible is not a collection of myths or legends but a trustworthy record of God's interaction with humanity. By examining these discoveries, we can gain greater confidence in the accuracy and truth of the biblical text.

CHAPTER 4 How Reliable Is the Old Testament?

The Divine Inspiration and Authority of the Old Testament

The Old Testament, also known as the Hebrew Scriptures, is foundational to the Christian faith, serving as the inspired, inerrant Word of God. According to 2 Timothy 3:16, "All Scripture is inspired by God and beneficial for teaching, for reproof, for correction, for training in righteousness." This verse highlights the divine inspiration of the Old Testament, ensuring its reliability and authority.

Furthermore, 2 Peter 1:21 states, "For no prophecy was ever made by an act of human will, but men moved by the Holy Spirit spoke from God." This emphasizes that the authors of the Old Testament were guided by the Holy Spirit, resulting in writings that are both accurate and authoritative. The divine inspiration guarantees that the Old Testament is a trustworthy record of God's revelation to humanity.

The Historical Accuracy of the Patriarchal Narratives

The accounts of the patriarchs—Abraham, Isaac, Jacob, and Joseph—are central to the Old Testament and have been supported by various archaeological discoveries. The Nuzi Tablets, dating back to the 15th century B.C.E., provide insight into the customs and legal practices of the ancient Near East, which align with the biblical narratives. For instance, the adoption of heirs, inheritance rights of women, and the significance of household gods, as seen in Genesis, are corroborated by these tablets (Genesis 15:2-4; Genesis 31:19).

The city of Ur, identified as Abraham's birthplace (Genesis 11:31), has been excavated, revealing a sophisticated civilization with advanced architecture and a wealth of cultural artifacts. These findings support the biblical account of Abraham's departure from a prosperous city to follow God's call.

Evidence of the Exodus and Conquest

The Exodus is a seminal event in Israel's history. While direct archaeological evidence of the Israelites' presence in Egypt and their subsequent exodus is limited, several discoveries provide indirect support. The Brooklyn Papyrus, dating to around 1740 B.C.E., lists the names of slaves in Egypt, many of which are Semitic, indicating the presence of a significant Semitic population during the period traditionally associated with the Israelites' enslavement.

The Merneptah Stele, dating to around 1208 B.C.E., contains the earliest extra-biblical reference to Israel, stating that "Israel is laid waste, his seed is not." This inscription confirms that a people known as Israel were present in Canaan during the late 13th century B.C.E., shortly after the traditional date of the Exodus around 1446 B.C.E.

Excavations at Jericho have revealed evidence of a city that was destroyed and subsequently abandoned during the late Bronze Age, which aligns with the biblical account of Joshua's conquest (Joshua 6:20-21). The discovery of collapsed walls and a layer of ash suggests a violent destruction, supporting the narrative of the walls falling after the Israelites' assault.

The United Monarchy: David and Solomon

The existence of King David and his dynasty has been a topic of debate among scholars. However, the discovery of the Tel Dan Stele in 1993 provided the first extra-biblical evidence of David's dynasty. The stele, dating to the 9th century B.C.E., contains an Aramaic inscription referring to the "House of David." This discovery confirms the biblical account of David's rule and his significance in Israel's history (1 Samuel 16:13; 2 Samuel 5:3-4).

Solomon's reign, described as a period of great prosperity and building projects, is also supported by archaeological findings. Excavations at Megiddo, Hazor, and Gezer have uncovered structures that match the description of Solomon's building activities in 1 Kings 9:15. These include gates and fortifications that reflect a centralized and powerful administration consistent with Solomon's kingdom.

Evidence from the Divided Kingdoms

IS THE BIBLE REALLY THE WORD OF GOD?

The period of the divided kingdoms of Israel and Judah is well-documented archaeologically. The Mesha Stele, also known as the Moabite Stone, dates to the 9th century B.C.E. and recounts the rebellion of King Mesha of Moab against Israel, as described in 2 Kings 3:4-27. This stele corroborates the biblical account of the conflict between Moab and Israel, providing a valuable historical context.

The Lachish Reliefs, found in the palace of Sennacherib at Nineveh, depict the Assyrian siege and conquest of Lachish in 701 B.C.E., an event recorded in 2 Kings 18:13-14. These reliefs provide a detailed visual representation of the siege, confirming the biblical narrative of the Assyrian invasion during King Hezekiah's reign.

The Babylonian Exile and Return

The Babylonian exile, a significant event in Jewish history, is also supported by archaeological evidence. The Babylonian Chronicles, a series of clay tablets, describe the conquest of Jerusalem by Nebuchadnezzar II in 597 B.C.E., as recorded in 2 Kings 24:10-14. These tablets confirm the biblical account of the fall of Jerusalem and the deportation of its inhabitants to Babylon.

The Cyrus Cylinder, an ancient clay artifact, contains an edict from King Cyrus of Persia, allowing exiled peoples, including the Jews, to return to their homelands and rebuild their temples. This decree, issued in 539 B.C.E., aligns with the biblical account of Cyrus's proclamation in 2 Chronicles 36:22-23 and Ezra 1:1-4, confirming the historical accuracy of the Jewish return from exile.

The Consistency and Coherence of the Old Testament Text

The Old Testament, written over a span of more than a thousand years, exhibits remarkable consistency and coherence. Despite being composed by different authors in various cultural and historical contexts, the Old Testament maintains a unified message centered on God's covenant relationship with His people.

The discovery of the Dead Sea Scrolls, which include portions of almost every book of the Hebrew Bible, has demonstrated the faithful transmission of the biblical text over centuries. The Great Isaiah Scroll, dating to around 150 B.C.E., matches closely with the Masoretic Text, illustrating the meticulous care taken by scribes in copying the Scriptures. This consistency underscores the reliability of the Old Testament as a trustworthy record of divine revelation.

The Prophetic Accuracy of the Old Testament

The fulfillment of Old Testament prophecies provides compelling evidence of its divine inspiration and reliability. For example, the prophecy in Isaiah 53, written around 700 B.C.E., vividly describes the suffering and atoning death of the Messiah, which Christians believe was fulfilled in Jesus Christ. Isaiah 53:5 states, "But he was pierced through for our transgressions, he was crushed for our iniquities; the chastening for our well-being fell upon him, and by his scourging we are healed." The precise fulfillment of this prophecy in the life and crucifixion of Jesus, as recorded in the New Testament, underscores the prophetic accuracy of the Old Testament.

Moreover, the prophecies concerning the rise and fall of empires, such as those found in Daniel 2 and 7, have been historically validated. Daniel 2:44 predicts the establishment of an eternal kingdom by God, which Christians interpret as the Kingdom of God inaugurated by Jesus. These fulfilled prophecies demonstrate the Bible's accuracy and divine foreknowledge, further establishing its reliability.

The Role of Faith and Reason

While historical, archaeological, and manuscript evidence provide strong support for the Old Testament's reliability, faith also plays a crucial role in accepting its divine authority. Hebrews 11:1 defines faith as "the assurance of things hoped for, the conviction of things not seen." This assurance is not blind belief but is based on reasonable evidence and the internal witness of the Holy Spirit.

Christian apologetics bridges the gap between faith and reason, demonstrating that believing in the Old Testament is intellectually viable and spiritually enriching. As 1 Peter 3:15 exhorts, "But sanctify Christ as Lord in your hearts, always being ready to make a defense to everyone who asks you to give an account for the hope that is in you, yet with gentleness and reverence." This call to defend the faith underscores the importance of understanding and articulating the reasons for trusting the Old Testament.

IS THE BIBLE REALLY THE WORD OF GOD?

Addressing Common Objections

Common objections to the Old Testament's reliability often stem from misunderstandings or misinterpretations of the text. For example, some critics argue that the presence of miracles in the Old Testament undermines its credibility. However, miracles, by definition, are extraordinary events that signify divine intervention. The parting of the Red Sea, the manna in the wilderness, and other miracles described in the Old Testament serve to demonstrate God's power and faithfulness to His people (Exodus 14:21-22; Exodus 16:4-5).

Another objection concerns the perceived contradictions in the Old Testament. A careful study using the Historical-Grammatical method of interpretation reveals that these apparent contradictions often result from a lack of understanding of the cultural, historical, and linguistic context. When properly interpreted, the Old Testament's messages are coherent and consistent, reinforcing its reliability.

The Importance of a Literal Interpretation

A literal interpretation of the Old Testament, using the Historical-Grammatical method, ensures that the text is understood as intended by its original authors. This approach respects the genre, historical context, and grammatical structure of the biblical writings, avoiding the pitfalls of subjective interpretations. As stated in Nehemiah 8:8, "They read from the book, from the law of God, translating to give the sense so that they understood the reading." This approach seeks to uncover the original meaning and apply it faithfully to contemporary contexts.

Literal Bible chronology, for example, provides a clear framework for understanding the timeline of biblical events. By adhering to the literal dates given in Scripture, such as the creation of the world around 4,000 B.C.E. and the Exodus around 1446 B.C.E., believers can align historical events with biblical narratives, enhancing the coherence and reliability of the Old Testament.

The Role of the Spirit-Inspired Word of God

It is essential to understand that Christians are guided by the Spirit-inspired Word of God rather than an indwelling of the Holy

Spirit. As John 16:13 applies only to the apostles, we rely on the Old Testament for guidance and understanding. The Scriptures provide the necessary wisdom and instruction for living a life pleasing to God. Psalm 119:105 states, "Your word is a lamp to my feet and a light to my path," highlighting the Old Testament's role in guiding believers.

The Testimony of Jesus and the Apostles

Jesus Christ and the apostles affirmed the reliability and authority of the Old Testament. In Matthew 5:18, Jesus stated, "For truly I say to you, until heaven and earth pass away, not the smallest letter or stroke shall pass from the Law until all is accomplished." Jesus' affirmation of the Old Testament underscores its divine authority and reliability. His fulfillment of Old Testament prophecies and His teachings further validate the truth of the Scriptures.

The apostles also consistently referenced the Old Testament to support their teachings and to demonstrate the fulfillment of prophecy in Jesus Christ. For instance, Peter's sermon on the day of Pentecost in Acts 2 cites the prophet Joel and the Psalms to explain the outpouring of the Holy Spirit and the resurrection of Jesus (Acts 2:16-36). This reliance on the Old Testament by Jesus and the apostles reinforces its reliability and centrality to the Christian faith.

CHAPTER 5 How Reliable Is the New Testament?

Divine Inspiration and Authority of the New Testament

The reliability of the New Testament is rooted in its divine inspiration. According to 2 Timothy 3:16, "All Scripture is inspired by God and beneficial for teaching, for reproof, for correction, for training in righteousness." This passage asserts that the New Testament, along with the Old Testament, is God-breathed, ensuring its authority and trustworthiness. The divine inspiration guarantees that the teachings and events recorded in the New Testament are accurate and reliable.

2 Peter 1:21 reinforces this understanding: "For no prophecy was ever made by an act of human will, but men moved by the Holy Spirit spoke from God." The authors of the New Testament were guided by the Holy Spirit, ensuring that their writings were free from error and conveyed God's intended message. This divine involvement underscores the New Testament's reliability as a faithful record of God's revelation.

Manuscript Evidence and Textual Integrity

The New Testament boasts an unparalleled wealth of manuscript evidence, which attests to its textual reliability. With over 5,800 Greek manuscripts, 10,000 Latin manuscripts, and thousands more in other languages, the New Testament has more ancient copies than any other ancient text. This abundance of manuscripts allows scholars to compare and reconstruct the original text with a high degree of confidence.

One notable manuscript is the Codex Sinaiticus, dating to the 4th century C.E. It contains the entire New Testament and demonstrates remarkable consistency with other ancient manuscripts. The consistency among these manuscripts underscores the careful transmission of the New Testament text over centuries. Textual criticism, the scholarly practice of comparing these manuscripts, has confirmed that the variations among them are minor and do not affect core Christian doctrines.

Eyewitness Testimony and Early Composition

The New Testament's reliability is further supported by the fact that many of its books were written by eyewitnesses or those who had direct access to eyewitnesses of Jesus' life and ministry. The Gospels of Matthew, Mark, Luke, and John, as well as the letters of Paul, Peter, James, and John, were composed within the first century C.E., within the lifetime of those who had witnessed the events they describe.

Luke, in the introduction to his Gospel, states, "Inasmuch as many have undertaken to compile an account of the things accomplished among us, just as they were handed down to us by those who from the beginning were eyewitnesses and servants of the word, it seemed fitting for me as well, having investigated everything carefully from the beginning, to write it out for you in consecutive order, most excellent Theophilus; so that you may know the exact truth about the things you have been taught" (Luke 1:1-4). This emphasis on careful investigation and reliance on eyewitness testimony enhances the credibility of the New Testament accounts.

Archaeological Corroboration

Archaeological discoveries have consistently supported the historical reliability of the New Testament. One significant find is the Pilate Stone, discovered in Caesarea Maritima, which bears the name of Pontius Pilate, the Roman governor who sentenced Jesus to crucifixion. This stone, dating to the 1st century C.E., provides independent confirmation of Pilate's existence and his role in the New Testament narrative (Matthew 27:2; John 19:1).

The Pool of Bethesda, mentioned in John 5:2 as the site where Jesus healed a paralytic, has been excavated in Jerusalem. The discovery of this pool, with its five porticoes, matches the description given in the Gospel of John, providing further evidence for the accuracy of the New Testament narratives.

The Reliability of Luke as a Historian

IS THE BIBLE REALLY THE WORD OF GOD?

The Gospel of Luke and the Acts of the Apostles, both written by Luke, have been validated through numerous archaeological findings. Sir William Ramsay, a renowned archaeologist, initially doubted the historical accuracy of Luke's writings. However, after extensive research and excavations in Asia Minor, Ramsay concluded that Luke was a highly reliable historian. Luke's precise descriptions of geographical locations, political titles, and cultural practices have been consistently confirmed by archaeological evidence.

In Acts 17:6-8, Luke refers to city officials in Thessalonica as "politarchs," a term not found in classical literature. Archaeological discoveries, including an inscription on an arch in Thessalonica, have since confirmed the use of this title in the first century C.E., affirming Luke's accuracy. This demonstrates that the New Testament's historical details are reliable and corroborated by external evidence.

The Consistency and Coherence of the New Testament Text

The New Testament, written over a span of several decades by multiple authors, exhibits remarkable consistency and coherence. Despite being composed by different authors in various cultural and historical contexts, the New Testament maintains a unified message centered on the life, death, and resurrection of Jesus Christ.

This consistency is particularly evident in the fulfillment of Old Testament prophecies. For instance, the prophecy in Isaiah 53, written around 700 B.C.E., vividly describes the suffering and atoning death of the Messiah, which Christians believe was fulfilled in Jesus Christ. Isaiah 53:5 states, "But he was pierced through for our transgressions, he was crushed for our iniquities; the chastening for our well-being fell upon him, and by his scourging we are healed." The precise fulfillment of this prophecy in the life and crucifixion of Jesus, as recorded in the New Testament, underscores the prophetic accuracy of the Bible.

The Prophetic Accuracy of the New Testament

The New Testament contains numerous prophecies that have been fulfilled, further attesting to its reliability. Jesus' prediction of the destruction of the Jerusalem Temple, recorded in Matthew 24:1-2, was fulfilled in 70 C.E. when the Roman army, led by Titus, destroyed the temple. This accurate prophecy underscores the divine foreknowledge and reliability of Jesus' words.

Moreover, the prophecies concerning the spread of the Gospel and the growth of the early church, as recorded in Acts, have been historically validated. Jesus' commission to His disciples in Acts 1:8, "But you will receive power when the Holy Spirit has come upon you; and you shall be My witnesses both in Jerusalem, and in all Judea and Samaria, and even to the remotest part of the earth," has been fulfilled as the message of Christianity spread throughout the Roman Empire and beyond.

Addressing Common Objections

Common objections to the New Testament's reliability often stem from misunderstandings or misinterpretations of the text. For example, some critics argue that the presence of miracles in the New Testament undermines its credibility. However, miracles, by definition, are extraordinary events that signify divine intervention. The resurrection of Jesus, a central miracle in Christianity, is supported by historical evidence and eyewitness testimonies, as recorded in 1 Corinthians 15:3-8.

Another objection concerns the perceived contradictions in the New Testament. A careful study using the Historical-Grammatical method of interpretation reveals that these apparent contradictions often result from a lack of understanding of the cultural, historical, and linguistic context. When properly interpreted, the New Testament's messages are coherent and consistent, reinforcing its reliability.

The Importance of a Literal Interpretation

A literal interpretation of the New Testament, using the Historical-Grammatical method, ensures that the text is understood as intended by its original authors. This approach respects the genre, historical context, and grammatical structure of the biblical writings, avoiding the pitfalls of subjective interpretations. As stated in Nehemiah 8:8, "They read from the book, from the law of God, translating to give the sense so that they understood the reading." This approach seeks to uncover the original meaning and apply it faithfully to contemporary contexts.

IS THE BIBLE REALLY THE WORD OF GOD?

Literal Bible chronology, for example, provides a clear framework for understanding the timeline of biblical events. By adhering to the literal dates given in Scripture, such as the death and resurrection of Jesus around 30 C.E. and the writing of the New Testament books within the first century C.E., believers can align historical events with biblical narratives, enhancing the coherence and reliability of the New Testament.

The Role of the Spirit-Inspired Word of God

It is essential to understand that Christians are guided by the Spirit-inspired Word of God rather than an indwelling of the Holy Spirit. As John 16:13 applies only to the apostles, we rely on the New Testament for guidance and understanding. The Scriptures provide the necessary wisdom and instruction for living a life pleasing to God. Psalm 119:105 states, "Your word is a lamp to my feet and a light to my path," highlighting the New Testament's role in guiding believers.

The Testimony of Jesus and the Apostles

Jesus Christ and the apostles affirmed the reliability and authority of the New Testament. In Matthew 5:18, Jesus stated, "For truly I say to you, until heaven and earth pass away, not the smallest letter or stroke shall pass from the Law until all is accomplished." Jesus' affirmation of the Scriptures underscores their divine authority and reliability. His fulfillment of Old Testament prophecies and His teachings further validate the truth of the New Testament.

The apostles consistently referenced the Old Testament to support their teachings and to demonstrate the fulfillment of prophecy in Jesus Christ. For instance, Peter's sermon on the day of Pentecost in Acts 2 cites the prophet Joel and the Psalms to explain the outpouring of the Holy Spirit and the resurrection of Jesus (Acts 2:16-36). This reliance on the Scriptures by Jesus and the apostles reinforces their reliability and centrality to the Christian faith.

Edward D. Andrews

CHAPTER 6 Did the Miracles Really Happen?

The Nature of Biblical Miracles

Miracles in the Bible are extraordinary events that manifest divine intervention in the natural world. They are not mere anomalies but are purposeful acts that reveal God's power and authority. The Bible consistently portrays miracles as signs and wonders that authenticate God's message and messengers. For example, in John 20:30-31, it is written, "Therefore many other signs Jesus also performed in the presence of the disciples, which are not written in this book; but these have been written so that you may believe that Jesus is the Christ, the Son of God; and that believing you may have life in His name." This passage highlights the purpose of miracles in affirming the identity and mission of Jesus Christ.

Old Testament Miracles: Evidence of Divine Power

The Old Testament is replete with miracles that demonstrate Jehovah's sovereignty over creation. One of the most significant collections of miracles is found in the account of the Exodus. The plagues in Egypt, culminating in the parting of the Red Sea, are prime examples. Exodus 14:21-22 describes this miraculous event: "Then Moses stretched out his hand over the sea; and Jehovah swept the sea back by a strong east wind all night and turned the sea into dry land, so the waters were divided. The sons of Israel went through the midst of the sea on the dry land, and the waters were like a wall to them on their right hand and on their left." This miracle served to deliver the Israelites from bondage and to demonstrate God's power over nature and nations.

The provision of manna in the wilderness is another significant miracle. In Exodus 16:14-15, the Bible records, "When the layer of dew evaporated, behold, on the surface of the wilderness there was a fine flake-like thing, fine as the frost on the ground. When the sons of Israel saw it, they said to one another, 'What is it?' For they did not know what it was. And Moses said to them, 'It is the bread which Jehovah has given you to eat.'" This daily provision for forty years sustained the Israelites and evidenced God's continual care and miraculous provision.

Miracles of Elijah and Elisha

The prophetic ministries of Elijah and Elisha are marked by numerous miracles that affirmed their divine calling and message. In 1 Kings 18:38-39, Elijah's contest with the prophets of Baal on Mount Carmel culminates in a dramatic miracle: "Then the fire of Jehovah fell and consumed the burnt offering and the wood and the stones and the dust, and licked up the water that was in the trench. When all the people saw it, they fell on their faces; and they said, 'Jehovah, He is God; Jehovah, He is God.'" This miracle validated Elijah's message and demonstrated the power of Jehovah over false gods.

Elisha, Elijah's successor, performed miracles that similarly authenticated his prophetic ministry. In 2 Kings 4:32-35, Elisha raises the Shunammite woman's son from the dead: "When Elisha came into the house, behold the lad was dead and laid on his bed. So he entered and shut the door behind them both and prayed to Jehovah. And he went up and lay on the child and put his mouth on his mouth and his eyes on his eyes and his hands on his hands, and he stretched himself on him; and the flesh of the child became warm. Then he returned and walked in the house once back and forth, and went up and stretched himself on him; and the lad sneezed seven times and the lad opened his eyes." This resurrection miracle affirmed Elisha's role as a prophet and God's power over life and death.

New Testament Miracles: Signs of the Messiah

The New Testament records numerous miracles performed by Jesus, which serve as signs of His messianic identity and divine authority. In Matthew 14:25-27, Jesus walks on water: "And in the fourth watch of the night He came to them, walking on the sea. When the disciples saw Him walking on the sea, they were terrified and said, 'It is a ghost!' And they cried out in fear. But immediately Jesus spoke to them, saying, 'Take courage, it is I; do not be afraid.'" This miracle demonstrates Jesus' mastery over the natural elements and His divine nature.

One of the most significant miracles in the New Testament is the resurrection of Lazarus, recorded in John 11:43-44: "When He had said these things, He cried out with a loud voice, 'Lazarus, come forth.' The man who had died came forth, bound hand and foot with wrappings, and his face was wrapped around with a cloth. Jesus said to them, 'Unbind him, and let him go.'" This miracle not only foreshadows Jesus' own resurrection but also serves as a powerful testament to His authority over life and death.

The resurrection of Jesus Christ is the cornerstone miracle of the Christian faith. As recorded in Matthew 28:5-7, the angel at the tomb announces, "Do not be afraid; for I know that you are looking for Jesus who has been crucified. He is not here, for He has risen, just as He said. Come, see the place where He was lying. Go quickly and tell His disciples that He has risen from the dead; and behold, He is going ahead of you into Galilee, there you will see Him; behold, I have told you." The resurrection is the ultimate validation of Jesus' divine identity and the guarantee of eternal life for believers.

Apostolic Miracles: Continuing the Mission

The apostles continued to perform miracles after Jesus' ascension, demonstrating the ongoing power of God through the early church. In Acts 3:6-8, Peter heals a lame man: "But Peter said, 'I do not possess silver and gold, but what I do have I give to you: In the name of Jesus Christ the Nazarene—walk!' And seizing him by the right hand, he raised him up; and immediately his feet and his ankles were strengthened. With a leap he stood upright and began to walk; and he entered the temple with them, walking and leaping and praising God." This miracle not only brought physical healing but also served as a sign to the people of the divine authority and power at work in the apostles.

Another significant miracle is the raising of Tabitha (Dorcas) from the dead by Peter, as recorded in Acts 9:40-41: "But Peter sent them all out and knelt down and prayed, and turning to the body, he said, 'Tabitha, arise.' And she opened her eyes, and when she saw Peter, she sat up. And he gave her his hand and raised her up; and calling the saints and widows, he presented her alive." This resurrection miracle affirmed Peter's apostolic authority and the power of Jesus' name even after His ascension.

The Purpose and Verification of Miracles

Biblical miracles serve specific purposes: they authenticate God's messengers, demonstrate divine authority, and provide tangible evidence of God's intervention in human history. Miracles are not random acts but are intentional and meaningful, often accompanied by a message or teaching that points to a greater spiritual truth. For instance, in John 9:3, Jesus explains the purpose of a man's blindness and subsequent healing: "It was neither that this man sinned, nor his parents; but it was so that the works of God might be displayed in him." The miracle not only restored the man's sight but also revealed the works and glory of God.

The historical reliability of the miracles recorded in the Bible is supported by the consistency and coherence of the biblical narratives, the early composition of the New Testament texts, and the willingness of the apostles and early Christians to suffer and die for their testimony. The resurrection of Jesus, in particular, is attested by multiple independent sources, including the Gospels and the letters of Paul. In 1 Corinthians 15:3-8, Paul provides a summary of the resurrection appearances, emphasizing the eyewitness nature of these accounts: "For I delivered to you as of first importance what I also received, that Christ died for our sins according to the Scriptures, and that He was buried, and that He was raised on the third day according to the Scriptures, and that He appeared to Cephas, then to the twelve. After that He appeared to more than five hundred brethren at one time, most of whom remain until now, but some have fallen asleep; then He appeared to James, then to all the apostles; and last of all, as to one untimely born, He appeared to me also." The numerous eyewitnesses and the transformation of the apostles from fearful followers to bold proclaimers of the resurrection provide compelling evidence for the historicity of this central miracle.

The Role of Faith and Reason

While the historical and textual evidence for biblical miracles is substantial, faith also plays a crucial role in accepting their reality.

Hebrews 11:1 defines faith as "the assurance of things hoped for, the conviction of things not seen." Faith in the miraculous works of God is not blind belief but is grounded in the reasonable evidence provided by Scripture and the internal witness of the Holy Spirit. The miracles recorded in the Bible invite believers to trust in the God who transcends natural laws and intervenes in human history for His purposes.

Christian apologetics bridges the gap between faith and reason, demonstrating that belief in biblical miracles is intellectually viable and spiritually enriching. As 1 Peter 3:15 exhorts, "But sanctify Christ as Lord in your hearts, always being ready to make a defense to everyone who asks you to give an account for the hope that is in you, yet with gentleness and reverence." This call to defend the faith includes providing reasons for believing in the miracles recorded in the Bible, emphasizing their role in revealing God's character and redemptive plan.

Addressing Skepticism and Misunderstandings

Skepticism regarding biblical miracles often arises from a naturalistic worldview that denies the possibility of supernatural intervention. However, a theistic worldview, which acknowledges the existence of an omnipotent God, provides a rational basis for the occurrence of miracles. If God created the universe and its natural laws, He is not bound by those laws and can intervene in extraordinary ways.

Some skeptics argue that the accounts of miracles in the Bible are mythical or symbolic rather than historical. However, the Historical-Grammatical method of interpretation, which seeks to understand the text in its original context and meaning, supports the literal understanding of these miraculous events. The detailed and consistent nature of the biblical narratives, along with the cultural and historical context provided by archaeological findings, reinforces the historicity of the miracles.

The Transformative Power of Miracles

The miracles recorded in the Bible are not only historical events but also carry profound spiritual significance. They reveal God's compassion, power, and desire to restore and redeem His creation. The healing miracles of Jesus, for instance, demonstrate His compassion for the suffering and His authority over sickness and death. In Matthew 9:35-36, it is written, "Jesus was going through all the cities and villages, teaching in their synagogues and proclaiming the gospel of the kingdom, and healing every kind of disease and every kind of sickness. Seeing the people, He felt compassion for them, because they were distressed and dispirited like sheep without a shepherd."

The miracles of provision, such as the feeding of the five thousand in John 6:1-14, reveal God's ability to meet the needs of His people. In this account, Jesus multiplies five barley loaves and two fish to feed a large crowd, illustrating God's abundant provision and care. These miracles serve as reminders of God's faithfulness and His ability to provide for His people's physical and spiritual needs.

Miracles as Foretastes of the Kingdom

The miracles performed by Jesus and the apostles are also seen as foretastes of the coming Kingdom of God. They provide glimpses of the future restoration and renewal that God has promised. In Revelation 21:4, it is prophesied, "And He will wipe away every tear from their eyes; and there will no longer be any death; there will no longer be any mourning, or crying, or pain; the first things have passed away." The miracles recorded in the Bible point forward to this ultimate restoration, offering hope and assurance to believers.

Conclusion on Miracles' Reality

The miracles recorded in the Bible are historically reliable and theologically significant. They are acts of divine intervention that reveal God's power, authenticate His messengers, and provide tangible evidence of His redemptive work. The Historical-Grammatical method of interpretation supports the literal understanding of these miracles, and the substantial historical and textual evidence corroborates their occurrence. Faith in biblical miracles is both reasonable and enriching, inviting believers to trust in the God who transcends natural laws and intervenes in human history for His purposes.

Edward D. Andrews

CHAPTER 7 Did Jesus Really Exist?

Historical Evidence for Jesus Christ

The question of Jesus Christ's historical existence has been extensively examined, and a wealth of evidence confirms His presence in history. The Gospels of Matthew, Mark, Luke, and John provide detailed accounts of Jesus' life, ministry, death, and resurrection. These accounts were written by eyewitnesses or those who had direct access to eyewitnesses, ensuring the reliability of their narratives.

External historical sources also affirm Jesus' existence. The Jewish historian Flavius Josephus, writing in the late first century C.E., refers to Jesus in his work "Antiquities of the Jews." Josephus writes, "Now there was about this time Jesus, a wise man, if it be lawful to call him a man, for he was a doer of wonderful works, a teacher of such men as receive the truth with pleasure." This passage confirms Jesus' historical existence and His reputation as a wise teacher and miracle worker.

Testimony from Roman Historians

Roman historians also provide independent confirmation of Jesus' existence. Tacitus, a Roman senator and historian, wrote about the persecution of Christians by Nero in his work "Annals." In this account, Tacitus refers to "Christus," who "suffered the extreme penalty during the reign of Tiberius at the hands of one of our procurators, Pontius Pilate." This reference aligns with the Gospel accounts of Jesus' crucifixion under Pilate, providing external validation from a non-Christian source.

Suetonius, another Roman historian, mentioned Christians and "Chrestus" in his work "The Twelve Caesars," referring to disturbances in Rome caused by followers of Christ. These references from Roman sources, written within a century of Jesus' life, corroborate the New Testament accounts and affirm Jesus' historical presence.

Archaeological Evidence Supporting the New Testament

Archaeological discoveries have also supported the historical reliability of the New Testament accounts of Jesus. The discovery of the Pilate Stone in Caesarea Maritima provides tangible evidence of Pontius Pilate, the Roman governor who sentenced Jesus to crucifixion. This stone, inscribed with Pilate's name and title, confirms the Gospel accounts of his role in Jesus' trial and execution (Matthew 27:2; John 19:1).

The Pool of Bethesda, where Jesus healed a paralytic (John 5:2), has been excavated in Jerusalem. The discovery of this pool, with its five porticoes, matches the description given in the Gospel of John, providing further evidence for the accuracy of the New Testament narratives.

Eyewitness Testimony in the New Testament

The New Testament is grounded in eyewitness testimony, which is crucial for establishing historical reliability. The Gospels were written by individuals who either witnessed the events themselves or recorded the accounts of those who did. Luke, in the introduction to his Gospel, states, "Inasmuch as many have undertaken to compile an account of the things accomplished among us, just as they were handed down to us by those who from the beginning were eyewitnesses and servants of the word, it seemed fitting for me as well, having investigated everything carefully from the beginning, to write it out for you in consecutive order, most excellent Theophilus; so that you may know the exact truth about the things you have been taught" (Luke 1:1-4).

The apostle Peter emphasizes the importance of eyewitness testimony in 2 Peter 1:16, where he writes, "For we did not follow cleverly devised tales when we made known to you the power and coming of our Lord Jesus Christ, but we were eyewitnesses of His majesty." This emphasis on firsthand accounts underscores the credibility of the New Testament documents.

The Consistency of the Gospel Accounts

The Gospels of Matthew, Mark, Luke, and John provide harmonious accounts of Jesus' life and ministry, despite being written by different authors for different audiences. The consistency among these accounts, particularly in the core events of Jesus' birth, miracles, teachings, crucifixion, and resurrection, reinforces their reliability. While there are variations in detail, these differences reflect the distinct perspectives and purposes of the authors rather than contradictions.

The synoptic Gospels—Matthew, Mark, and Luke—share many similarities, often recounting the same events in similar sequences. This synoptic relationship suggests a common source or tradition, further affirming the historical reliability of their accounts. The Gospel of John, while more theological in nature, corroborates the synoptic accounts and provides additional insights into Jesus' ministry and teachings.

The Early Composition of the New Testament

The New Testament documents were written within the first century C.E., within the lifetime of those who witnessed Jesus' ministry. This early composition is crucial for historical reliability, as it minimizes the potential for legendary development or distortion of the original events. Paul's letters, some of the earliest New Testament writings, date to the 50s C.E., just two to three decades after Jesus' crucifixion.

The early date of the New Testament writings is supported by the lack of mention of the destruction of Jerusalem in 70 C.E. in the synoptic Gospels. Given the significance of this event, its absence suggests that these Gospels were composed before the destruction, likely in the 60s C.E. This proximity to the actual events enhances the credibility of the New Testament accounts.

Testimony from Early Christian Writings

The writings of early church fathers provide additional testimony to Jesus' existence and the reliability of the New Testament. Clement of Rome, writing around 95 C.E., refers to Jesus' teachings and the resurrection in his letter to the Corinthians. Ignatius of Antioch, writing in the early second century, also affirms Jesus' crucifixion and resurrection in his letters to various churches.

These early Christian writings demonstrate the continuity and consistency of the Christian faith from its inception. They also reflect the widespread acceptance of the New Testament accounts as accurate records of Jesus' life and ministry.

The Martyrdom of the Apostles

The willingness of the apostles to suffer and die for their testimony is a powerful testament to the reliability of their accounts. According to tradition, all the apostles, except John, were martyred for their faith. Their willingness to face persecution and death rather than renounce their testimony suggests that they genuinely believed in the truth of their message.

Peter, for instance, was crucified upside down, as recorded by early church tradition. Paul was beheaded in Rome under Emperor Nero. These accounts of martyrdom highlight the apostles' unwavering commitment to their testimony, providing strong evidence for the reliability of their witness.

Non-Christian Sources Confirming Jesus' Existence

In addition to Jewish and Roman sources, other non-Christian writings also reference Jesus. The Talmud, a central text of Rabbinic Judaism, mentions Jesus in a few passages, albeit with a hostile tone. These references, despite their negative portrayal, affirm Jesus' historical existence and His impact on Jewish society.

Pliny the Younger, a Roman governor, wrote to Emperor Trajan around 112 C.E., describing how Christians worshiped Christ "as to a god." This correspondence indicates the spread of Christianity and the recognition of Jesus as a central figure of worship, further attesting to His historical existence.

Addressing Skepticism and Alternative Theories

Skepticism regarding Jesus' historical existence often arises from a naturalistic worldview that denies the possibility of the supernatural. Some skeptics argue that the accounts of Jesus are mythical or symbolic rather than historical. However, the Historical-Grammatical method of interpretation, which seeks to understand the text in its original context and meaning, supports the literal understanding of Jesus' existence and the events recorded in the New Testament.

Alternative theories, such as the Christ myth theory, which posits that Jesus is a fictional or mythological figure, lack substantial historical evidence and are not widely accepted by scholars. The overwhelming consensus among historians, both Christian and non-Christian, is that Jesus of Nazareth was a historical figure who lived in the first century C.E.

The Impact of Jesus' Life and Teachings

The historical impact of Jesus' life and teachings provides further evidence of His existence. Jesus' teachings on love, forgiveness, and the Kingdom of God have profoundly influenced Western civilization and continue to shape ethical and moral thought. The rapid growth of the early Christian church, despite intense persecution, testifies to the powerful impact of Jesus' message and the conviction of His followers.

The spread of Christianity from a small group of Jewish disciples to a global faith within a few centuries underscores the historical reality of Jesus and the transformative power of His teachings. The early church's commitment to preserving and disseminating the New Testament writings reflects their belief in the historical accuracy and significance of these documents.

The Role of Faith and Reason

While historical and textual evidence for Jesus' existence is substantial, faith also plays a crucial role in accepting His identity and message. Hebrews 11:1 defines faith as "the assurance of things hoped for, the conviction of things not seen." Faith in Jesus Christ is not blind belief but is grounded in reasonable evidence provided by Scripture and the internal witness of the Holy Spirit.

Christian apologetics bridges the gap between faith and reason, demonstrating that belief in Jesus' historical existence and His divine identity is intellectually viable and spiritually enriching. As 1 Peter 3:15 exhorts, "But sanctify Christ as Lord in your hearts, always being ready to make a defense to everyone who asks you to give an account for the hope that is in you, yet with gentleness and reverence." This call to defend the faith includes providing reasons for believing in the historical reality of Jesus Christ.

CHAPTER 8 The Resurrection of Jesus, Did It Really Happen?

The Centrality of the Resurrection in Christian Faith

The resurrection of Jesus Christ is the cornerstone of Christian faith. As Paul asserts in 1 Corinthians 15:14, "and if Christ has not been raised, then our preaching is vain, your faith also is vain." This statement underscores the essential nature of the resurrection; without it, Christianity loses its foundational claim. The resurrection is not only a demonstration of Jesus' divine power but also the guarantee of eternal life for believers, affirming His victory over sin and death.

Eyewitness Testimonies and Early Creeds

The New Testament provides multiple accounts of Jesus' resurrection, grounded in eyewitness testimonies. These accounts are recorded in the Gospels and the letters of Paul, which were written within the first century C.E., close to the actual events. Paul, in 1 Corinthians 15:3-8, offers a summary of the resurrection appearances: "For I delivered to you as of first importance what I also received, that Christ died for our sins according to the Scriptures, and that He was buried, and that He was raised on the third day according to the Scriptures, and that He appeared to Cephas, then to the twelve. After that He appeared to more than five hundred brethren at one time, most of whom remain until now, but some have fallen asleep; then He appeared to James, then to all the apostles; and last of all, as to one untimely born, He appeared to me also."

This passage highlights the variety and number of witnesses who claimed to have seen the risen Jesus, providing a robust foundation for the resurrection narrative. The mention of over five hundred witnesses, many of whom were still alive at the time of Paul's writing, invites contemporaneous verification of the claims.

The Empty Tomb

The empty tomb is a critical piece of evidence for the resurrection. All four Gospels attest to the discovery of the empty tomb by women followers of Jesus (Matthew 28:1-7; Mark 16:1-8; Luke 24:1-12; John 20:1-10). The fact that women, whose testimony was considered less credible in the first-century Jewish context, are reported as the primary witnesses to the empty tomb lends credibility to the accounts. If the story were fabricated, it is unlikely that women would be depicted as the first witnesses.

The empty tomb alone does not prove the resurrection, but it is a significant part of the cumulative case. The Jewish and Roman authorities had every reason to produce Jesus' body to quash the burgeoning Christian movement, yet no body was ever produced. The absence of Jesus' body from the tomb remains a compelling mystery that points towards the resurrection.

Post-Resurrection Appearances

The New Testament records multiple post-resurrection appearances of Jesus to His disciples and others. These appearances are described with specific details and locations, such as Jesus' encounter with Mary Magdalene (John 20:11-18), His appearance to the disciples on the road to Emmaus (Luke 24:13-35), and His meeting with Thomas (John 20:24-29). These accounts provide consistency and coherence across the various narratives, reinforcing the claim of the resurrection.

Moreover, the transformation of the disciples from a group of frightened, disillusioned followers into bold proclaimers of the resurrection is noteworthy. The disciples were willing to face persecution and death for their testimony, suggesting they genuinely believed in the risen Jesus. As Peter declared in Acts 2:32, "This Jesus God raised up again, to which we are all witnesses." This bold proclamation, made in Jerusalem where the events occurred, adds to the credibility of their witness.

The Conversion of Paul

IS THE BIBLE REALLY THE WORD OF GOD?

One of the most compelling pieces of evidence for the resurrection is the conversion of Paul. Originally a fierce persecutor of Christians, Paul experienced a dramatic transformation after encountering the risen Jesus on the road to Damascus (Acts 9:1-19). This encounter led Paul to become one of the most ardent defenders and spreaders of the Christian faith.

In his letters, Paul repeatedly cites the resurrection as the cornerstone of his message. In Galatians 1:11-12, he writes, "For I would have you know, brethren, that the gospel which was preached by me is not according to man. For I neither received it from man, nor was I taught it, but I received it through a revelation of Jesus Christ." Paul's dramatic shift from persecutor to apostle, driven by his encounter with the risen Christ, provides strong evidence for the resurrection.

The Growth of the Early Church

The rapid growth of the early Christian church in the face of intense persecution is another testament to the reality of the resurrection. The apostles and early Christians proclaimed the resurrection despite facing severe opposition from both Jewish and Roman authorities. The willingness of early Christians to suffer and die for their faith suggests they truly believed in the resurrection.

The Book of Acts documents the explosive growth of the early church, attributing it to the power of the resurrection message. In Acts 4:33, it states, "And with great power the apostles were giving testimony to the resurrection of the Lord Jesus, and abundant grace was upon them all." The resilience and expansion of the Christian faith in its nascent stages underscore the transformative impact of the resurrection.

External Historical Sources

External historical sources from non-Christian writers also provide evidence for the resurrection and the existence of early Christians. Tacitus, a Roman historian, wrote about the persecution of Christians under Nero and mentioned Christus (Christ) who "suffered the extreme penalty during the reign of Tiberius at the hands of one of our procurators, Pontius Pilate." This aligns with the New Testament accounts of Jesus' crucifixion and the subsequent growth of the Christian movement.

Josephus, a first-century Jewish historian, also references Jesus and His followers. In his work "Antiquities of the Jews," Josephus writes, "At this time there was a wise man who was called Jesus. And his conduct was good, and he was known to be virtuous. And many people from among the Jews and the other nations became his disciples. Pilate condemned him to be crucified and to die. But those who had become his disciples did not abandon his discipleship. They reported that he had appeared to them three days after his crucifixion and that he was alive."

While some aspects of the Josephus passage are disputed, its core affirmations about Jesus, His crucifixion under Pilate, and the persistent belief in His resurrection among His followers are significant.

Addressing Common Objections

Skeptics often raise objections to the resurrection, including claims that the disciples stole Jesus' body or that the resurrection appearances were hallucinations. However, these theories fail to account for the historical and textual evidence adequately.

The theory that the disciples stole the body is implausible given their initial despair and fear following Jesus' crucifixion. The transformation of the disciples into bold proclaimers of the resurrection, willing to face persecution and death, argues against the idea that they fabricated the resurrection.

The hallucination theory also falls short. Hallucinations are typically individual and subjective experiences, yet the New Testament records multiple group appearances of the risen Jesus. Paul mentions that Jesus appeared to over five hundred people at once (1 Corinthians 15:6), a phenomenon not consistent with psychological explanations of hallucinations.

The Theological Significance of the Resurrection

The resurrection of Jesus is not only a historical event but also a theological cornerstone. It validates Jesus' claims about His identity and mission. Jesus' resurrection is the fulfillment of Old Testament prophecies and the guarantee of believers' future resurrection. In Romans 4:25, Paul writes, "He who was delivered over because of our transgressions, and was raised because of our justification." The resurrection signifies God's approval of Jesus' sacrificial death and His power to grant eternal life.

Moreover, the resurrection provides hope and assurance for Christians. In 1 Peter 1:3-4, it is written, "Blessed be the God and Father of our Lord Jesus Christ, who according to His great mercy has caused us to be born again to a living hope through the resurrection of Jesus Christ from the dead, to obtain an inheritance which is imperishable and undefiled and will not fade away, reserved in heaven for you." This living hope, grounded in the historical reality of the resurrection, sustains believers in their faith and life.

Faith and Reason in the Resurrection

While the historical and textual evidence for the resurrection is substantial, faith also plays a crucial role in accepting its reality. Hebrews 11:1 defines faith as "the assurance of things hoped for, the conviction of things not seen." Faith in the resurrection is not blind belief but is grounded in reasonable evidence provided by Scripture and the internal witness of the Holy Spirit.

Christian apologetics bridges the gap between faith and reason, demonstrating that belief in the resurrection is intellectually viable and spiritually enriching. As 1 Peter 3:15 exhorts, "But sanctify Christ as Lord in your hearts, always being ready to make a defense to everyone who asks you to give an account for the hope that is in you, yet with gentleness and reverence." This call to defend the faith includes providing reasons for believing in the historical reality of the resurrection.

Edward D. Andrews

CHAPTER 9 What about the Mistakes, Errors, And Contradictions in the Bible?

The Nature of Biblical Inerrancy

The doctrine of biblical inerrancy asserts that the Bible, in its original manuscripts, is without error in all that it affirms. This belief is grounded in the understanding that the Scriptures are divinely inspired. As 2 Timothy 3:16 states, "All Scripture is inspired by God and beneficial for teaching, for reproof, for correction, for training in righteousness." The term "inspired by God" literally means "God-breathed," indicating that the Scriptures originate from God Himself. Consequently, they are trustworthy and reliable.

Moreover, 2 Peter 1:21 reinforces the divine origin of Scripture: "For no prophecy was ever made by an act of human will, but men moved by the Holy Spirit spoke from God." This passage highlights that the human authors of the Bible wrote under the guidance of the Holy Spirit, ensuring that their writings were free from error. The inerrancy of the Bible, therefore, is not a claim about every copy or translation but about the original autographs.

Alleged Contradictions and Contextual Clarifications

Critics often point to alleged contradictions in the Bible to challenge its inerrancy. However, many of these supposed contradictions can be resolved through a careful examination of the context, language, and cultural background. The Historical-Grammatical method of interpretation, which seeks to understand the text as the original audience would have, is particularly useful in addressing these issues.

For example, consider the accounts of Judas Iscariot's death in Matthew 27:5 and Acts 1:18. Matthew states, "And he threw the pieces of silver into the temple sanctuary and departed; and he went away and hanged himself." Acts, however, records, "Now this man acquired a field with the price of his wickedness, and falling headlong, he burst open in the middle and all his intestines gushed out." At first glance, these accounts appear contradictory. However, they can be harmonized by understanding that both events could have occurred: Judas hanged himself, and after his body decomposed, it fell and burst open. This explanation respects the integrity of both passages without forcing a contradiction.

Variations in Gospel Accounts

The Gospels of Matthew, Mark, Luke, and John sometimes present variations in their accounts of Jesus' life and ministry. These differences are often cited as contradictions. However, it is important to recognize that each Gospel writer had a unique perspective and purpose, which influenced their selection and presentation of events.

For instance, the synoptic Gospels (Matthew, Mark, and Luke) record Jesus cleansing the temple towards the end of His ministry (Matthew 21:12-13; Mark 11:15-17; Luke 19:45-46), while John places a similar event at the beginning (John 2:13-16). One plausible explanation is that Jesus cleansed the temple twice, once at the beginning of His ministry and once towards the end. Alternatively, John may have arranged his Gospel thematically rather than chronologically, focusing on the significance of the event rather than its exact timing.

Numerical Discrepancies

Numerical discrepancies are another area where critics claim the Bible contains errors. A well-known example is the differing numbers of fighting men in Israel as reported in 2 Samuel 24:9 and 1 Chronicles 21:5. 2 Samuel 24:9 states, "And Joab gave the number of the registration of the people to the king; and there were in Israel eight hundred thousand valiant men who drew the sword, and the men of Judah were five hundred thousand men." In contrast, 1 Chronicles 21:5 reports, "And Joab gave the number of the census of all the people to David. And all Israel were one million one hundred thousand men who drew the sword, and Judah was four hundred and seventy thousand men who drew the sword."

Several factors could account for this difference. It is possible that the numbers were rounded or that different methods of counting were used. Another explanation is that the Chronicler included additional groups of soldiers not counted in Samuel's account. These variations do not undermine the overall reliability of the biblical narrative but reflect the complexity of ancient record-keeping practices.

Scribal Errors and Textual Variants

Over centuries of transmission, scribal errors and textual variants have inevitably occurred in the manuscripts of the Bible. These errors include misspellings, duplications, and omissions. However, the discipline of textual criticism allows scholars to compare thousands of manuscripts to reconstruct the original text with a high degree of confidence.

One famous example is the so-called "Johannine Comma" in 1 John 5:7-8. The King James Version includes the phrase "in heaven: the Father, the Word, and the Holy Ghost: and these three are one. And there are three that bear witness in earth." However, this phrase is absent from the earliest Greek manuscripts and is widely considered a later addition. Modern translations, based on more reliable manuscripts, omit this phrase. Such textual variants, while notable, do not affect the core doctrines of the Christian faith and are identified and addressed through scholarly research.

Harmonizing Difficult Passages

Many alleged contradictions can be harmonized by understanding the historical and cultural context of the passages. For instance, the different genealogies of Jesus presented in Matthew 1 and Luke 3 have been cited as a contradiction. Matthew traces Jesus' lineage through David's son Solomon, while Luke traces it through David's son Nathan. A common explanation is that Matthew records Joseph's genealogy, emphasizing Jesus' legal right to David's throne, while Luke records Mary's genealogy, emphasizing Jesus' biological descent from David.

Another example is the differing accounts of the death of King Saul. 1 Samuel 31:4 states that Saul took his own life by falling on his sword, while 2 Samuel 1:10 records an Amalekite claiming to have killed Saul at his request. One plausible explanation is that Saul attempted to take his own life but did not die immediately, and the Amalekite, finding him mortally wounded, finished the task. This harmonization respects both accounts and resolves the apparent discrepancy.

Understanding Literary Genres and Devices

The Bible employs various literary genres and devices, including poetry, parable, and hyperbole, which must be interpreted accordingly. Recognizing these genres helps clarify passages that might otherwise be misunderstood as contradictions or errors. For example, Jesus' statement in Matthew 5:29, "If your right eye makes you stumble, tear it out and throw it from you," is clearly hyperbolic, emphasizing the severity of sin rather than prescribing literal self-mutilation.

Similarly, the imprecatory psalms, such as Psalm 137:9, "How blessed will be the one who seizes and dashes your little ones against the rock," express intense emotions and desires for justice in poetic form. Understanding these as expressions of human anguish and calls for divine justice, rather than literal prescriptions for action, resolves potential ethical dilemmas.

The Role of Faith and Reason in Addressing Difficulties

While historical, contextual, and textual analyses address many alleged contradictions and errors, faith also plays a crucial role in accepting the reliability of the Bible. Hebrews 11:1 defines faith as "the assurance of things hoped for, the conviction of things not seen." Faith in the Bible's inerrancy is not blind belief but is grounded in the reasonable evidence provided by Scripture and the internal witness of the Holy Spirit.

Christian apologetics bridges the gap between faith and reason, demonstrating that belief in the Bible's inerrancy is intellectually viable and spiritually enriching. As 1 Peter 3:15 exhorts, "But sanctify Christ as Lord in your hearts, always being ready to make a defense to everyone who asks you to give an account for the hope that is in you, yet with gentleness and reverence." This call to defend the faith includes addressing challenges to the Bible's reliability with well-reasoned responses.

The Witness of Jesus and the Apostles

The testimony of Jesus and the apostles provides additional assurance of the Bible's reliability. Jesus affirmed the authority and reliability of the Old Testament, stating in Matthew 5:18, "For truly I say to you, until heaven and earth pass away, not the smallest letter or stroke shall pass from the Law until all is accomplished." Jesus' endorsement of the Scriptures as trustworthy and enduring underscores their divine origin and reliability.

The apostles also affirmed the reliability of Scripture. Peter, in 2 Peter 1:16-21, emphasizes the prophetic nature of Scripture and its divine inspiration. Paul, in 2 Timothy 3:16, asserts the usefulness and divine origin of all Scripture. These affirmations from Jesus and the apostles reinforce the Christian conviction that the Bible is the inerrant Word of God.

Addressing Ethical and Scientific Challenges

Some critics argue that the Bible contains ethical or scientific errors, challenging its reliability. However, many of these challenges arise from misunderstandings of the Bible's purpose and genre. The Bible is not a scientific textbook but a theological and historical document that conveys spiritual truths through various literary forms.

For example, the creation accounts in Genesis are often critiqued for their perceived conflict with modern scientific understandings. However, the purpose of these accounts is not to provide a scientific explanation of the origins of the universe but to convey theological truths about God's creative power and the relationship between God and creation. Recognizing the genre and intent of these passages helps reconcile perceived conflicts with scientific knowledge.

Ethical challenges, such as the Bible's depiction of violence or its treatment of women and slavery, must be understood in their historical and cultural context. The Bible records the realities of ancient societies and God's redemptive work within those contexts. While certain practices described in the Bible reflect the cultural norms of the time, the overarching biblical narrative reveals God's progressive revelation of justice, mercy, and love.

IS THE BIBLE REALLY THE WORD OF GOD?

The Consistency and Coherence of the Biblical Narrative

Despite being written over a span of 1,500 years by more than 40 authors from diverse backgrounds, the Bible exhibits remarkable consistency and coherence. This unity is evident in the overarching narrative of creation, fall, redemption, and restoration that runs throughout the Scriptures. The consistency of themes, prophecies, and teachings across different books and authors points to the divine inspiration of the Bible.

For example, the prophecy of the suffering servant in Isaiah 53, written around 700 B.C.E., finds its fulfillment in the New Testament account of Jesus' crucifixion. Isaiah 53:5 states, "But he was pierced through for our transgressions, he was crushed for our iniquities; the chastening for our well-being fell upon him, and by his scourging we are healed." The precise fulfillment of this prophecy in the life and death of Jesus underscores the coherence and reliability of the biblical narrative.

Conclusion on the Inerrancy of the Bible

The Bible, in its original manuscripts, is the inerrant and inspired Word of God. Alleged contradictions and errors can often be resolved through careful examination of the context, language, and literary genres. The Historical-Grammatical method of interpretation, along with textual criticism, provides robust tools for understanding and defending the reliability of the Scriptures. Faith in the Bible's inerrancy is grounded in reasonable evidence and the testimony of Jesus and the apostles, demonstrating that the Bible is a trustworthy and reliable revelation of God's truth.

Edward D. Andrews

CHAPTER 10 Has Science Proved the Bible Wrong?

The Relationship Between Science and Scripture

The relationship between science and Scripture is often perceived as one of conflict. However, when both are properly understood, they can be seen as complementary rather than contradictory. The Bible is primarily a theological and historical document, revealing God's interaction with humanity and His plan of salvation. Science, on the other hand, seeks to understand the natural world through observation and experimentation. When interpreted correctly, both Scripture and scientific findings can coexist harmoniously.

2 Timothy 3:16 states, "All Scripture is inspired by God and beneficial for teaching, for reproof, for correction, for training in righteousness." This verse underscores the divine origin and purpose of the Bible, which is to provide spiritual and moral guidance rather than detailed scientific explanations. Similarly, Psalm 19:1 declares, "The heavens are telling of the glory of God; and their expanse is declaring the work of His hands." This acknowledges that the natural world reveals God's majesty and power, suggesting that scientific discoveries about creation can enhance our understanding of the Creator.

The Bible and Cosmology

One of the most significant areas of perceived conflict between the Bible and science is cosmology—the study of the origins and structure of the universe. Critics often point to the biblical creation account in Genesis as being at odds with the Big Bang theory and the age of the universe.

Genesis 1:1 states, "In the beginning God created the heavens and the earth." This foundational verse aligns with the concept that the universe had a definitive beginning, a view supported by modern cosmology through the Big Bang theory. While the Bible does not provide a scientific account of creation, it affirms that the universe was purposefully created by God.

The age of the universe, estimated by scientists to be around 13.8 billion years, is often seen as conflicting with a literal interpretation of the Genesis creation days as 24-hour periods. However, many conservative evangelical scholars interpret the "days" of Genesis 1 as creative periods of unspecified length, allowing for an old earth view that is consistent with scientific evidence. This interpretation aligns with 2 Peter 3:8, which states, "But do not let this one fact escape your notice, beloved, that with the Lord one day is like a thousand years, and a thousand years like one day," emphasizing that God's perspective on time differs from human perception.

The Bible and Biology

Another area of perceived conflict is the origin of life and the theory of evolution. The Bible's account of creation in Genesis describes God creating distinct kinds of living organisms, culminating in the creation of human beings in His image (Genesis 1:26-27). This account is often contrasted with the scientific theory of evolution, which posits that all life forms evolved from common ancestors through natural selection.

While we reject theistic evolution as unbiblical, it is important to emphasize that the Bible's primary purpose is to reveal God's relationship with humanity, rather than to provide a detailed scientific explanation of biological processes. The account of creation should be understood as a series of creative periods during which God brought various forms of life into existence.

Psalm 139:13-14 highlights the intimate and purposeful creation of human beings: "For You formed my inward parts; You wove me in my mother's womb. I will give thanks to You, for I am fearfully and wonderfully made; wonderful are Your works, and my soul knows it very well." This passage emphasizes the theological truth that humans are created with purpose and dignity by a loving Creator, a truth that remains regardless of the specific mechanisms of biological development.

The Bible's Insights into Science

The Bible, though not a scientific textbook, contains insights and statements that align with scientific discoveries made thousands of years later. These insights demonstrate the advanced understanding of natural phenomena in the Scriptures, providing further evidence of their divine inspiration.

Fixity of Kinds: "According to Their Kinds"

Genesis 1 repeatedly uses the phrase "according to their kinds" to describe the creation of plants and animals. This phrase implies a fixity of kinds, suggesting that distinct types of organisms were created separately and do not evolve into entirely different kinds. Modern biology recognizes the stability of species' genetic boundaries, affirming the biblical account of fixed kinds.

Astronomy: Stars and the Vast Universe

The Bible's description of the stars and the universe reflects an advanced understanding of astronomy. Genesis 22:17 states, "Indeed I will greatly bless you, and I will greatly multiply your seed as the stars of the heavens and as the sand which is on the seashore." Jeremiah 33:22 echoes this, saying, "As the host of heaven cannot be counted and the sand of the sea cannot be measured, so I will multiply the descendants of David My servant and the Levites who minister to Me." These verses acknowledge the immense number of stars, a fact confirmed by modern astronomy, which estimates billions of galaxies, each containing billions of stars.

Earth's Position and Shape

Isaiah 40:22 states, "It is He who sits above the circle of the earth, and its inhabitants are like grasshoppers, who stretches out the heavens like a curtain and spreads them out like a tent to dwell in." This reference to the "circle of the earth" aligns with the understanding that the earth is spherical, a fact not commonly accepted until much later in history.

Job 26:7 provides further insight into the earth's position in space: "He stretches out the north over empty space and hangs the earth on nothing." This description accurately portrays the earth as suspended in space, a concept that aligns with modern astronomical understanding.

Earth's Perfect "Address"

The Bible implicitly acknowledges the fine-tuning of the universe to support life on earth. The specific conditions necessary for life—such as the earth's distance from the sun, its orbital path, and the presence of a stable atmosphere—are seen as a result of divine design. This fine-tuning is highlighted in passages like Psalm 104:5, which states, "He established the earth upon its foundations, so that it will not totter forever and ever." The precision required for these conditions aligns with modern scientific recognition of the fine-tuning of the universe.

The Atmosphere and Photosynthesis

Isaiah 45:18 declares, "For thus says Jehovah, who created the heavens (He is the God who formed the earth and made it, He established it and did not create it a waste place, but formed it to be inhabited), 'I am Jehovah, and there is none else.'" This verse underscores the earth's suitability for habitation, which includes the presence of an atmosphere that supports life.

The process of photosynthesis, essential for life on earth, is a testament to the intricate design of creation. Psalm 104:14 acknowledges the role of plants in sustaining life: "He causes the grass to grow for the cattle, and vegetation for the labor of man, so that he may bring forth food from the earth." The understanding that plants convert sunlight into energy, providing the basis for the food chain, reflects the wisdom of the Creator.

Self-Reproducing Cells and Complexity of Life

The complexity of life, from the self-reproducing cell to the human body, points to intelligent design. The Bible emphasizes the intentional and intricate creation of life. Job 10:8-12 speaks to this complexity: "Your hands fashioned and made me altogether, and would You destroy me? Remember now, that You have made me as clay; and would You turn me into dust again? Did You not pour me out like milk and curdle me like cheese; clothe me with skin and flesh, and knit me together with bones and sinews? You have granted me life and lovingkindness; and Your care has preserved my spirit." This poetic description highlights the complexity and wonder of human creation, aligning with modern biological understanding of the intricacies of life.

Natural Cycles for Life

Ecclesiastes 1:7 observes, "All the rivers flow into the sea, yet the sea is not full. To the place where the rivers flow, there they flow again." This statement reflects an understanding of the water cycle, which is essential for sustaining life on earth. The continuous movement of water through evaporation, condensation, and precipitation is a fundamental natural process recognized by science.

Earth's Protective Shields

The Bible also alludes to the protective features of the earth. Psalm 47:9 states, "The princes of the peoples have assembled themselves as the people of the God of Abraham, for the shields of the earth belong to God; He is highly exalted." This can be seen as a metaphorical reference to the earth's protective shields, such as the magnetic field and the ozone layer, which protect life from harmful solar radiation and cosmic rays.

The Role of Faith and Reason

While scientific discoveries can enhance our understanding of God's creation, faith ultimately plays a crucial role in accepting the Bible as the authoritative Word of God. Hebrews 11:1 defines faith as "the assurance of things hoped for, the conviction of things not seen." Faith in the reliability of Scripture is not contrary to reason but is supported by reasonable evidence and the internal witness of the Holy Spirit.

Christian apologetics bridges the gap between faith and reason, demonstrating that belief in the Bible is intellectually viable and spiritually enriching. As 1 Peter 3:15 exhorts, "But sanctify Christ as Lord in your hearts, always being ready to make a defense to everyone who asks you to give an account for the hope that is in you, yet with gentleness and reverence." This call to defend the faith includes providing well-reasoned answers to challenges regarding the relationship between the Bible and science.

The Testimony of Jesus and the Apostles

The testimony of Jesus and the apostles provides additional assurance of the Bible's reliability. Jesus affirmed the authority and reliability of the Old Testament, stating in Matthew 5:18, "For truly I say to you, until heaven and earth pass away, not the smallest letter or stroke shall pass from the Law until all is accomplished." Jesus' endorsement of the Scriptures as trustworthy and enduring underscores their divine origin and reliability.

The apostles also affirmed the reliability of Scripture. Peter, in 2 Peter 1:16-21, emphasizes the prophetic nature of Scripture and its divine inspiration. Paul, in 2 Timothy 3:16, asserts the usefulness and divine origin of all Scripture. These affirmations from Jesus and the apostles reinforce the Christian conviction that the Bible is the inerrant Word of God.

Addressing Ethical and Scientific Challenges

Some critics argue that the Bible contains ethical or scientific errors, challenging its reliability. However, many of these challenges arise from misunderstandings of the Bible's purpose and genre. The Bible is not a scientific textbook but a theological and historical document that conveys spiritual truths through various literary forms.

For example, the creation accounts in Genesis are often critiqued for their perceived conflict with modern scientific understandings. However, the purpose of these accounts is not to provide a scientific explanation of the origins of the universe but to convey theological truths about God's creative power and the relationship between God and creation. Recognizing the genre and intent of these passages helps reconcile perceived conflicts with scientific knowledge.

Ethical challenges, such as the Bible's depiction of violence or its treatment of women and slavery, must be understood in their historical and cultural context. The Bible records the realities of ancient societies and God's redemptive work within those contexts. While certain practices described in the Bible reflect the cultural norms of the time, the overarching biblical narrative reveals God's progressive revelation of justice, mercy, and love.

The Consistency and Coherence of the Biblical Narrative

Despite being written over a span of 1,500 years by more than 40 authors from diverse backgrounds, the Bible exhibits remarkable consistency and coherence. This unity is evident in the overarching narrative of creation, fall, redemption, and restoration that runs throughout the Scriptures. The consistency of themes, prophecies, and teachings across different books and authors points to the divine inspiration of the Bible.

For example, the prophecy of the suffering servant in Isaiah 53, written around 700 B.C.E., finds its fulfillment in the New Testament account of Jesus' crucifixion. Isaiah 53:5 states, "But he was pierced through for our transgressions, he was crushed for our iniquities; the chastening for our well-being fell upon him, and by his scourging we are healed." The precise fulfillment of this prophecy in the life and death of Jesus underscores the coherence and reliability of the biblical narrative.

Conclusion on the Compatibility of Science and Scripture

The Bible, when interpreted correctly, is not at odds with scientific discoveries. Alleged conflicts can often be resolved through a careful examination of the context, language, and literary genres of the biblical text. The Historical-Grammatical method of interpretation, along with a recognition of the distinct roles of science and Scripture, provides a robust framework for understanding the harmony between the two. Faith in the Bible's reliability is grounded in reasonable evidence and the testimony of Jesus and the apostles, demonstrating that the Bible is a trustworthy and reliable revelation of God's truth.

CHAPTER 11 How Can We Know That Any of the Prophecies Come True?

Understanding Biblical Prophecy

Biblical prophecy is a significant feature of Scripture, with many prophecies spanning from the Old Testament to the New Testament. Prophecy in the Bible is not merely about foretelling future events but also about conveying God's message to His people. As 2 Peter 1:21 states, "For no prophecy was ever made by an act of human will, but men moved by the Holy Spirit spoke from God." This emphasizes that biblical prophecies are divinely inspired and serve to reveal God's sovereign plan.

The Nature of Fulfilled Prophecies

The Bible contains numerous prophecies that have been fulfilled, providing strong evidence for its divine inspiration. Fulfilled prophecy is a unique characteristic of the Bible that sets it apart from other religious texts. The accuracy and specificity of these prophecies demonstrate that they are not the result of human guesswork but of divine revelation.

Messianic Prophecies

One of the most compelling areas of fulfilled prophecy is the Messianic prophecies—predictions about the coming of the Messiah, Jesus Christ. These prophecies, found throughout the Old Testament, were fulfilled in the life, death, and resurrection of Jesus, providing strong evidence for the reliability of Scripture.

Birthplace of the Messiah

The prophet Micah, writing around 700 B.C.E., foretold that the Messiah would be born in Bethlehem. Micah 5:2 states, "But as for you, Bethlehem Ephrathah, too little to be among the clans of Judah, from you One will go forth for Me to be ruler in Israel. His goings forth are from long ago, from the days of eternity." This prophecy was fulfilled in the birth of Jesus, as recorded in Matthew 2:1, "Now after Jesus was born in Bethlehem of Judea in the days of Herod the king, magi from the east arrived in Jerusalem."

The Virgin Birth

Isaiah 7:14 prophesied the virgin birth of the Messiah, "Therefore Jehovah Himself will give you a sign: Behold, a virgin will be with child and bear a son, and she will call His name Immanuel." This prophecy was fulfilled in the birth of Jesus, as described in Matthew 1:22-23, "Now all this took place to fulfill what was spoken by Jehovah through the prophet: 'Behold, the virgin shall be with child and shall bear a son, and they shall call His name Immanuel,' which translated means, 'God with us.'"

Betrayal for Thirty Pieces of Silver

Zechariah 11:12-13 predicted the betrayal of the Messiah for thirty pieces of silver, "I said to them, 'If it is good in your sight, give me my wages; but if not, never mind!' So they weighed out thirty shekels of silver as my wages. Then Jehovah said to me, 'Throw it to the potter, that magnificent price at which I was valued by them.' So I took the thirty shekels of silver and threw them to the potter in the house of Jehovah." This prophecy was fulfilled in the betrayal of Jesus by Judas Iscariot, as recorded in Matthew 26:14-15, "Then one of the twelve, named Judas Iscariot, went to the chief priests and said, 'What are you willing to give me to betray Him to you?' And they weighed out thirty pieces of silver to him."

Crucifixion Details

Psalm 22, written by David around 1000 B.C.E., contains several detailed prophecies about the crucifixion of the Messiah. Psalm 22:16-18 states, "For dogs have surrounded me; a band of evildoers has encompassed me; they pierced my hands and my feet. I can count all my bones. They look, they stare at me; they divide my garments among them, and for my clothing they cast lots." These details were fulfilled in the crucifixion of Jesus, as described in John 19:23-24, "Then the soldiers, when they had crucified Jesus, took His outer garments and made four parts, a part to every soldier and also the tunic; now the tunic was seamless, woven in one piece. So they said to one another, 'Let us not tear it, but cast lots for it, to decide whose it shall be.' This was to fulfill the Scripture: 'They divided My outer garments among them, and for My clothing they cast lots.'"

Resurrection Prophecy

The resurrection of Jesus was also prophesied in the Old Testament. Psalm 16:10 states, "For You will not abandon my soul to Sheol; nor will You allow Your Holy One to undergo decay." This prophecy was fulfilled in the resurrection of Jesus, as Peter explained in Acts 2:31-32, "he looked ahead and spoke of the resurrection of the Christ, that He was neither abandoned to Hades, nor did His flesh suffer decay. This Jesus God raised up again, to which we are all witnesses."

Prophecies Concerning Nations and Historical Events

The Bible also contains prophecies concerning nations and historical events that have been fulfilled with remarkable accuracy. These prophecies further attest to the divine inspiration of Scripture and its reliability.

Destruction of Tyre

The prophet Ezekiel, writing in the 6th century B.C.E., predicted the destruction of the city of Tyre. Ezekiel 26:3-14 describes how many nations would come against Tyre, its walls would be broken down, and it would become a bare rock. This prophecy was fulfilled through a series of events, beginning with the siege by Nebuchadnezzar of Babylon and later by Alexander the Great. The city of Tyre was ultimately destroyed and remains in ruins to this day.

Fall of Babylon

Isaiah 13:19-22 prophesied the fall of Babylon, stating, "And Babylon, the beauty of kingdoms, the glory of the Chaldeans' pride, will be as when God overthrew Sodom and Gomorrah. It will never be inhabited or lived in from generation to generation." This prophecy was fulfilled when Babylon fell to the Medes and Persians in 539

B.C.E. The city, once a magnificent center of power, was eventually abandoned and lies in ruins, confirming the accuracy of the prophecy.

Return of Israel to the Land

The Bible contains numerous prophecies about the return of the Jewish people to their land. Isaiah 11:11-12 states, "Then it will happen on that day that Jehovah will again recover the second time with His hand the remnant of His people, who will remain, from Assyria, Egypt, Pathros, Cush, Elam, Shinar, Hamath, and from the islands of the sea. And He will lift up a standard for the nations and assemble the banished ones of Israel, and will gather the dispersed of Judah from the four corners of the earth." This prophecy has seen fulfillment in modern times with the establishment of the State of Israel in 1948 and the subsequent return of Jews from around the world.

Prophecies Concerning the End Times

The Bible also contains prophecies concerning the end times, many of which align with current global events, further validating the reliability of Scripture.

Global Increase in Knowledge and Travel

Daniel 12:4 predicts, "But as for you, Daniel, conceal these words and seal up the book until the end of time; many will go back and forth, and knowledge will increase." The rapid increase in knowledge and global travel in recent times aligns with this prophecy, suggesting its fulfillment in the modern era.

Moral Decline and Apostasy

2 Timothy 3:1-5 describes the moral decline that will characterize the last days, "But realize this, that in the last days difficult times will come. For men will be lovers of self, lovers of money, boastful, arrogant, revilers, disobedient to parents, ungrateful, unholy, unloving, irreconcilable, malicious gossips, without self-control, brutal, haters of good, treacherous, reckless, conceited, lovers of pleasure rather than lovers of God, holding to a form of godliness, although they have denied its power." Observations of contemporary society reveal many of these characteristics, indicating the potential fulfillment of this prophecy.

IS THE BIBLE REALLY THE WORD OF GOD?

The Role of Faith and Reason

While the fulfillment of biblical prophecies provides substantial evidence for the reliability of Scripture, faith also plays a crucial role in accepting these truths. Hebrews 11:1 defines faith as "the assurance of things hoped for, the conviction of things not seen." Faith in the Bible's prophecies is not contrary to reason but is supported by reasonable evidence and the internal witness of the Holy Spirit.

Christian apologetics bridges the gap between faith and reason, demonstrating that belief in the fulfillment of biblical prophecies is intellectually viable and spiritually enriching. As 1 Peter 3:15 exhorts, "But sanctify Christ as Lord in your hearts, always being ready to make a defense to everyone who asks you to give an account for the hope that is in you, yet with gentleness and reverence." This call to defend the faith includes providing well-reasoned answers to challenges regarding the fulfillment of biblical prophecies.

The Testimony of Jesus and the Apostles

The testimony of Jesus and the apostles provides additional assurance of the reliability of biblical prophecies. Jesus affirmed the fulfillment of prophecies concerning Himself, stating in Luke 24:44, "Now He said to them, 'These are My words which I spoke to you while I was still with you, that all things which are written about Me in the Law of Moses and the Prophets and the Psalms must be fulfilled.'" Jesus' fulfillment of Messianic prophecies validates their divine origin and accuracy.

The apostles also affirmed the fulfillment of prophecies. Peter, in Acts 2:16-21, cites the fulfillment of Joel's prophecy concerning the outpouring of the Holy Spirit on the day of Pentecost. Paul, in 1 Corinthians 15:3-4, emphasizes the fulfillment of prophecies regarding Christ's death and resurrection, "For I delivered to you as of first importance what I also received, that Christ died for our sins according to the Scriptures, and that He was buried, and that He was raised on the third day according to the Scriptures."

Addressing Skepticism and Misunderstandings

Skepticism regarding biblical prophecies often arises from misunderstandings or misinterpretations of the texts. Critics may argue that some prophecies are vague or self-fulfilling. However, many prophecies are highly specific and have been fulfilled in ways that could not have been orchestrated by human effort.

For example, the detailed prophecies concerning the life and ministry of Jesus, written centuries before His birth, could not have been fulfilled by chance or manipulation. The convergence of multiple prophecies in the person of Jesus Christ provides compelling evidence for their divine origin.

The Consistency and Coherence of Prophetic Fulfillment

Despite being written over a span of 1,500 years by more than 40 authors from diverse backgrounds, the Bible exhibits remarkable consistency and coherence in its prophetic fulfillment. This unity is evident in the overarching narrative of creation, fall, redemption, and restoration that runs throughout the Scriptures. The consistency of themes, prophecies, and teachings across different books and authors points to the divine inspiration of the Bible.

For example, the prophecy of the suffering servant in Isaiah 53, written around 700 B.C.E., finds its fulfillment in the New Testament account of Jesus' crucifixion. Isaiah 53:5 states, "But he was pierced through for our transgressions, he was crushed for our iniquities; the chastening for our well-being fell upon him, and by his scourging we are healed." The precise fulfillment of this prophecy in the life and death of Jesus underscores the coherence and reliability of the biblical narrative.

IS THE BIBLE REALLY THE WORD OF GOD?

CHAPTER 12 How Can We Explain So Many Bible Difficulties?

IT SEEMS THAT the charge that the Bible contradicts itself has been made more and more in the last 20 years. Generally, those making such claims are merely repeating what they have heard because most have not even read the Bible, let alone done an in-depth study of it. I do not wish, however, to set aside all concerns as though they have no merit. There are many who raise legitimate questions that seem, on the surface anyway, to be about well-founded contradiction. Sadly, these issues have caused many to lose their faith in God's Word, the Bible. The purpose of this chapter is, to help its readers to be able to defend the Bible against Bible critics (1 Pet. 3:15), to contend for the faith (Jude 1:3), and help those, who have begun to doubt. – Jude 1:22-23.

Before we begin explaining things, let us jump right in, getting our feet wet, and deal with two major Bible difficulties, so we can see that there are reasonable, logical answers. After that, we will delve deeper into explaining Bible difficulties.

Is God permitting Human Sacrifice?

Judges 11:29-34, 37-40? Updated American Standard Version (UASV)

²⁹ Then the Spirit of the Lord was upon Jephthah, and he passed through Gilead and Manasseh; and passed on to Mizpah of Gilead, and from Mizpah of Gilead he passed on to the sons of Ammon. ³⁰ And Jephthah **made a vow** to Jehovah and said, "If You will indeed give the sons of Ammon into my hand, ³¹ then it shall be that **whatever** comes out of the doors of my house to meet me when I return in peace from the sons of Ammon, it shall be Jehovah's, and I will offer it up as a burnt offering." ³² So Jephthah crossed over to the sons of Ammon to fight against them; and Jehovah gave them into his

hand. ³³ He struck them with a very great slaughter from Aroer as far as Minnith, twenty cities, and as far as Abel-keramim. So the sons of Ammon were subdued before the sons of Israel.

³⁴ When Jephthah came to his house at Mizpah, behold, **his daughter was coming out to meet him** with tambourines and with dancing. Now she was his one and only child; besides her he had no son or daughter.

³⁷ And she said to her father, "Let this thing be done for me: leave me alone two months, that I may go up and down on the mountains and weep because of my virginity, I and my companions." ³⁸ And he said, "Go." So he sent her away for two months; and **she left with her companions, and wept on the mountains because of her virginity**. ³⁹ At the end of two months she returned to her father, who **did to her according to the vow that he had made**; and she never known a man.¹ Thus it became a custom in Israel, ⁴⁰ that the daughters of Israel went year by year **to commemorate² the daughter** of Jephthah the Gileadite four days in the year.

It is true; to infer that having the idea of an animal sacrifice would really have not been an impressive vow, which the context requires. Human sacrifice will be repugnant if we are talking about taking a life. Jephthah had no sons, so he likely knew it was the daughter, who would come to greet him.

First, the text does not say he killed his daughter. The idea of some that he did kill her is concluded only by inference. While it is not good policy to interpret backward, using Paul on Judges, he does say humans are to be **"as a living sacrifice."** Therefore, Jephthah could have offered his daughter at the temple, "as a living sacrifice" in service, like Samuel.

This is not to be taken dismissively, because, under Jewish backgrounds, it is no small thing to offer a **perpetual virginity** as a sacrifice. This would mean Jephthah's lineage would not be carried on, the family name, was no more.

---

¹ I.e., *never had relations with a man*
² Or *lament*

IS THE BIBLE REALLY THE WORD OF GOD?

Second, the context says she went out to weep for two months, not mourn her death. It says, "she left with her companions, and **wept on the mountains because of her virginity."**

If she was facing imminent death, she could have married, and spent that last two months as a married woman. There would be absolutely no reason for her to mourn her virginity if she were not facing perpetual virginity. – Exodus 38:8; 1 Samuel 2:22

Third, it was completely forbidden to offer a human sacrifice. – Leviticus 18:21; 20:2-5; Deuteronomy 12:31; 18:10

Imagine an Israelite believing that he could please God with a human sacrifice that was intended to offer up a human life. To do so would have been a rejection of Jehovah's Sovereignty (the very person you are asking for help), and a rejection of the Law that made them a special people. Worse still, this interpretation would have us believe that Jehovah knew this was coming, allowed the vow, and then aided this type of man to succeed over his enemies.

The last point is simple enough. If such a man as one who would make such a vow, in gross violation of the law, and then carry it out; there is no way he would be mentioned by Paul in Hebrews chapter 11 among the most faithful men and women in Israelite history.

In review, there is no way God would have granted and helped in Jephthah's initial success knowing the vow that was coming because both Jehovah and Jephthah would be as bad as the Canaanites. There is no way that God would accept such a vow and then go on to help Jephthah with his enemies yet again. Then, to allow such a vow to be carried out, to then put Jephthah on the wall of star witnesses for God in Hebrews chapter 11.

Does Isaiah 45:7 mean that God Is the Author of Evil?

Isaiah 45:7 King James Version (KJV)	Isaiah 45:7 English Standard Version (ESV)
⁷ I form the light, and create darkness: I make peace, and **create evil**: I the Lord do all these things.	⁷ I form light and create darkness, I make well-being and **create calamity**, I am the Lord, who does all these things.[3]

Encarta Dictionary: (Evil) (1) morally bad: profoundly immoral or wrong (2) deliberately causing great harm, pain, or upset

QUESTION: Is this view of evil always the case? No, as you will see below.

Some apologetic authors try to say, 'we do not understand Isaiah 45:7 correctly, because there are other verses that say God is not evil (1 John 1:5), cannot look approvingly on evil (Hab. 1:13), and cannot be tempted by evil. (James 1:13)' Well, while all of these things are Scripturally true, the question at hand is not: Is God evil, can God approvingly look on evil, or can God be tempted with evil? Those questions are not relevant to the one at hand, as God cannot be those things, and at the same time, he can be the yes to our question. The question is, is God the author, the creator of evil?

We would hardly argue that God was **not just** in his bringing "calamity" or "evil" down on Adam and Eve. Thus, we have Isaiah 45:7 saying that God is the creator of "calamity" or "evil."

Let us begin simple, without trying to be philosophical. When God removed Adam and Eve from the Garden of Eden, he sentenced them and humanity to sickness, old age, and death. (Rom. 5:8; i.e., enforce penalty for sin), which was to bring "calamity" or "evil" upon humankind. Therefore, as we can see "evil" does not always mean wrongdoing. Other examples of God bringing "calamity" or "evil" are

---

[3] See Jeremiah 18:11, Lamentations 3:18, and Amos 3:6

IS THE BIBLE REALLY THE WORD OF GOD?

Noah and the flood, the Ten Plagues of Egypt, and the destruction of the Canaanites. These acts of evil were not acts of wrongdoing. Rather, they were righteous and just, because God, the Creator of all things, was administering justice to wrongdoers, to sinners. He warned the perfect first couple what the penalty was for sin. He warned the people for a hundred years by Noah's preaching. He warned the Canaanites centuries before.

Nevertheless, there are times, when God extends mercy, refraining from the execution of his righteous judgment to one worthy of calamity. For example, he warned Nineveh, the city of blood, and they repented, so he pardoned them. (Jonah 3:10) God has made it a practice to warn persons of the results of sin, giving them undeservedly many opportunities to change their ways. – Ezekiel 33:11.

God cannot sin; it is impossible for him to do so. So, when did he create evil? Without getting into the eternity of his knowing what he was going to do, and when, let us just say, evil did not exist when he was the only person in existence. We might say the idea of evil existed because he knew what he was going to do. However, the moment he created creatures (spirit and human), the potential for evil came into existence because both have free will to sin (fall short of perfection). Evil became a reality the moment Satan entertained the idea of causing Adam to sin, to get humanity for himself, and then acted on it.

God has the right and is just to bring the *calamity of* or *evil* down on anyone that is an unrepentant sinner. God did not even have to give us the underserved kindness of offering us his Son. God is the author or agent of evil regardless of the source books that claim otherwise. If he had never created free will beings, evil would have never gone from the idea of evil to the potential of evil, to the existence of evil. However, God felt that it was better to get the sinful state out of angel and human existence, recover, and then any who would sin thereafter; he would be justified in handing out evil or calamity to only that person or angel alone.

Who among us would argue that he should have created humans and angels like robots, automatons with no free will? The moment he chose the free will, he moved evil from an idea to a potential, and Satan moved it to reality. God has a moral nature that does not bring about evil and sin when he is the only person in existence. However, the moment he created beings in his image, which had the potential to sin, he brought about evil. The moment we have a moral code of good and evil that is placed upon one's with free will; then, we have evil as a potential.

In English, the very comprehensive Hebrew word ra' is variously translated as "bad," "downcast (sad, NASB)," "ugly," "evil," "grievous (distressing, NASB)," "sore," "selfish (stingy, HCSB)," and "envious," depending upon the context. (Gen 2:9; 40:7; 41:3; Ex 33:4; Deut. 6:22; 28:35; Pro 23:6; 28:22)

Evil as an adjective **describes** the **quality of** a class of people, places, or things, or of a specific person, place, or thing

Evil as a noun, **defines** the **nature** of a class of people, places, or things, or of a specific person, place, or thing (e.g., the evil one, evil eye).

We can agree that "evil" is a thing. Create means to bring something into existence, be it people, places, or things, as well something abstract, for lack of a better word at the moment. We would agree that when God was alone evil was not a reality; it did not exist? We would agree that the moment that God created free will creatures (angels and humans), creating humans in his image, with his moral nature, he also brought the potential for evil into existence, and it was realized by Satan?

Inerrancy: Can the Bible Be trusted?

If the Bible is the Word of God, it should be in complete agreement throughout; there should be no contradictions. Yet, the rational mind must ask, why is it that some passages appear to be contradictions when compared with others? For example, Numbers 25:9 tells us that 24,000 died from the scourge, whereas at 1 Corinthians 10:8, the apostle Paul says it was 23,000. This would seem to be a clear error. Before addressing such matters, let us first look at some background information.

Full inerrancy in this book means that the original writings are fully without error in all that they state, as are the words. The words were not dictated (automaton), but the intended meaning is inspired, as are the words that convey that meaning. The Author allowed the writer to use his style of writing, yet controlled the meaning to the extent of not allowing the writer to choose a wrong word, which would not convey the intended meaning. Other more liberal-minded persons hold with *partial inerrancy*, which claims that as far as faith is concerned, this portion of God's Word is without error, but that there are historical, geographical, and scientific errors.

There are several different levels of inerrancy. *Absolute Inerrancy* is the belief that the Bible is fully true and exact in every way; including not only relationships and doctrine, but also science and history. In other words, all information is completely exact. *Full Inerrancy* is the belief that the Bible was not written as a science or historical textbook, but is phenomenological, in that it is written from the human perspective. In other words, speaking of such things as the sun rising, the four corners of the earth or the rounding off of number approximations are all from a human perspective. *Limited Inerrancy* is the belief that the Bible is meant only as a reflection of God's purposes and will, so the science and history is the understanding of the author's day, and is limited. Thus, the Bible is susceptible to errors in these areas. *Inerrancy of Purpose* is the belief that it is only inerrant in the purpose of bringing its readers to a saving faith. The Bible is not about facts, but about persons and relationships, thus, it is subject to error. *Inspired: Not Inerrant* is the belief that its authors are human and thus subject to human error. It should be noted that this author holds the position of full inerrancy.

For many today, the Bible is nothing more than a book written by men. The Bible critic believes the Bible to be full of myths and legends, contradictions, and geographical, historical, and scientific errors. University professor Gerald A. Larue had this to say, "The views of the writers as expressed in the Bible reflect the ideas, beliefs, and concepts current in their own times and are limited by the extent of knowledge in those times."[4] On the other hand, the Bible's authors claim that their writings were inspired of God, as Holy Spirit moved

---

[4] Gerald Larue, "The Bible as a Political Weapon," *Free Inquiry* (Summer 1983): 39.

them along. We will discover shortly that the Bible critics have much to say, but it is inflated or empty.

2 Timothy 3:16-17 Updated American Standard Version (UASV)

¹⁶ All Scripture is inspired by God and profitable for teaching, for reproof, for correction, for training in righteousness; ¹⁷ so that the man of God may be fully competent, equipped for every good work.

2 Peter 1:21 Updated American Standard Version (UASV)

²¹ for no prophecy was ever produced by the will of man, but men carried along by the Holy Spirit spoke from God.

The question remains as to whether the Bible is a book written by imperfect men and full of errors, or is written by imperfect men, but inspired by God. If the Bible is just another book by imperfect man, there is no hope for humankind. If it is inspired by God and without error, although penned by imperfect men, we have the hope of everything that it offers: a rich, happy life now by applying counsel that lies within and the real life that is to come, everlasting life. This author contends that the Bible is inspired of God and free of human error, although written by imperfect humans.

Before we take on the critics who seem to sift the Scriptures looking for problematic verses, let us take a moment to reflect on how we should approach these alleged problem texts. The critic's argument goes something like this: 'If God does not err and the Bible is the Word of God, then the Bible should not have one single error or contradiction, yet it is full of errors and contradictions.' If the Bible is riddled with nothing but contradictions and errors as the critics would have us believe, why, out of 31,173 verses in the Bible, should there be only 2-3 thousand Bible difficulties that are called into question, this being less than ten percent of the whole?

First, let it be said that it is every Christian's obligation to get a deeper understanding of God's Word, just as the apostle Paul told Timothy:

1 Timothy 4:15-16 Updated American Standard Version (UASV)

¹⁵ Practice these things, be absorbed in them, so that your progress will be evident to all. ¹⁶ Pay close attention to yourself and to your

teaching; persevere in these things, for as you do this you will ensure salvation both for yourself and for those who hear you.

Paul also told the Corinthians:

2 Corinthians 10:4-5 Updated American Standard Version (UASV)

⁴ For the weapons of our warfare are not of the flesh[5] but powerful to God for destroying strongholds.[6] ⁵ We are destroying speculations and every lofty thing raised up against the knowledge of God, and we are taking every thought captive to the obedience of Christ,

Paul also told the Philippians:

Philippians 1:7 Updated American Standard Version (UASV)

⁷ It is right for me to feel thus about you all, because I hold you in my heart, for you are all partakers with me of grace, both in my imprisonment and in the defense and confirmation of the gospel.

In being able to defend against the modern-day critic, one has to be able to reason from the Scriptures and overturn the critic's argument(s) with mildness. If someone were to approach us about an alleged error or contradiction, what should we do? We should be frank and honest. If we do not have an answer, we should admit such. If the text in question gives the appearance of difficulty, we should admit this as well. If we are unsure as to how we should answer, we can simply say that we will look into it and get back to them, returning with a reasonable answer.

However, we do not want to express disbelief and doubt to our critics, because they will be emboldened in their disbelief. It will put them on the offense and us on the defense. With great confidence, we can express that there is an answer. The Bible has withstood the test of 2,000 years of persecution and interrogation and yet it is the most printed book of all time, currently being translated into 2,287

---

[5] That is *merely human*

[6] That is *tearing down false arguments*

languages. If these critical questions were so threatening, the Bible would not be the book that it is.

When we are pursuing the text in question, be unwavering in purpose, or resolved to find an answer. In some cases, it may take hours of digging to find the solution. Consider this: as we resolve these difficulties, we are also building our faith that God's Word is inerrant. Moreover, we will want to do preventative maintenance in our personal study. As we are doing our Bible reading, take note of these surface discrepancies and resolve them as we work our way through the Bible. We need to make this part of our prayers as well. I recommend the following program. Below are several books that deal with difficult passages. As we daily read and study our Bible from Genesis to Revelation, do not attempt it in one year; make it a four-year program. Use a good exegetical commentary like *The Holman Old/New Testament Commentary* (HOTC/HNTC) or *The New American Commentary* set, and *The Big Book of Bible Difficulties* by Norman L. Geisler, as well as *The Encyclopedia of Bible Difficulties* by Gleason Archer.

We should be aware that men under inspiration penned the originally written books. In fact, we do not have those originals, what textual scholars call autographs, but we do have thousands of copies. The copyists, however, were not inspired; therefore, as one might expect, throughout the first 1,400 years of copying, thousands of errors were transmitted into the texts that were being copied by imperfect hands that were not under inspiration when copying. Yet, the next 450 years saw a restoration of the text by textual scholars from around the world. Therefore, while many of our best literal translations today may not be inspired, they are a mirror-like reflection of the autographs by way of textual criticism.[7] Therefore, the fallacy could be with the copyist error that has simply not been weeded out. In addition, we must keep in mind that God's Word is without error, but our interpretation and understanding of that Word is not.

It should be noted that the Bible is made up of 66 smaller books that were hand-written over a period of 1,600 years, having some 40

---

[7] Textual criticism is the study of copies of any written work of which the autograph (original) is unknown, with the purpose of ascertaining the original text. Harold J. Green, Introduction to New Testament Textual Criticism (Peabody, MA: Hendrickson, 1995), 1.

writers of various trades such as shepherd, king, priest, tax collector, governor, physician, copyist, fisherman, and a tentmaker. Therefore, it should not surprise us that some difficulties are encountered as we casually read the Bible. Yet, if one were to take a deeper look, one would find that these difficulties are easily explained. Let us take a few pages to examine some passages that have been under attack.

This chapter's objective is not to be exhaustive, not even close. What we are looking to do is cover a few alleged contradictions and a couple of alleged mistakes. This is to give us a small sampling of the reasonable answers that we will find in the above recommended books. Remember, our Bible is a sword that we must use both offensively and defensively. One must wonder how long a warrior of ancient times would last who was not expertly trained in the use of his weapon. Let us look at a few scriptures that support our need to learn our Bible well so will be able to defend what we believe to be true.

When "false apostles, deceitful workmen, disguising themselves as apostles of Christ" were causing trouble in the congregation in Corinth, the apostle Paul wrote that under such circumstances, we are to *tear down their arguments* and *take every thought captive*. (2 Corinthians 10:4, 5; 11:13–15) All who present critical arguments against God's Word, or contrary to it, can have their arguments overturned by the Christian, who is able and ready to defend that Word in mildness. – 2 Timothy 2:24–26.

1 Peter 3:15 Updated American Standard Version (UASV)

[15] but sanctify Christ as Lord in your hearts, always being prepared to make a defense[8] to anyone who asks you for a reason for the hope that is in you; yet do it with gentleness and respect;

Peter says that we need to be prepared to make a *defense*. The Greek word behind the English 'defense' is *apologia*, which is actually a legal term that refers to the defense of a defendant in court. Our English apologetics is just what Peter spoke of, having the ability to give a reason to any who may challenge us, or to answer those who are

---

[8] Or *argument*; or *explanation*

not challenging us but who have honest questions that deserve to be answered.

2 Timothy 2:24-25 Updated American Standard Version (UASV)

²⁴ For a slave of the Lord does not need to fight, but needs to be kind to all, qualified to teach, showing restraint when wronged ²⁵ with gentleness correcting those who are in opposition, if perhaps God may grant them repentance leading to accurate knowledge[9] of the truth,

Look at the Greek word (*epignosis*) behind the English "knowledge" in the above. "It is more intensive than *gnosis* (1108), knowledge because it expresses a more thorough participation in the acquiring of knowledge on the part of the learner."[10] The requirement of all of the Lord's servants is that they be able to teach, but not in a quarrelsome way, and in a way to correct his opponents with mildness. Why? Because the purpose of it all is that by God, and through the Christian teacher, one may come to repentance and begin taking in an accurate knowledge of the truth.

Inerrancy: Practical Principles to Overcoming Bible Difficulties

Below are several ways of looking at the Bible that enable the reader to see he is not dealing with an error or contradiction, but rather a Bible difficulty.

Different Points of View

At times, you may have two different writers who are writing from two different points of view.

Numbers 35:14 Updated American Standard Version (UASV)

¹⁴ You shall give three cities across the Jordan and three cities you shall give in the land of Canaan; they will be cities of refuge.

---

[9] *Epignosis* is a strengthened or intensified form of *gnosis* (*epi*, meaning "additional"), meaning, "true," "real," "full," "complete" or "accurate," depending upon the context. Paul and Peter alone use *epignosis*.

[10] Spiros Zodhiates, *The Complete Word Study Dictionary: New Testament,* Electronic ed. (Chattanooga, TN: AMG Publishers, 2000, c1992, c1993), S. G1922.

IS THE BIBLE REALLY THE WORD OF GOD?

Joshua 22:4 Updated American Standard Version (UASV)

⁴ And now Jehovah your God has given rest to your brothers, as he spoke to them; therefore turn now and go to your tents, to the land of your possession, which Moses the servant of Jehovah gave you beyond the Jordan. [on the other side of the Jordan, ESV]

Here we see that Moses is speaking about the east side of the Jordan when he says "on this side of the Jordan." Joshua, on the other hand, is also speaking about the east side of the Jordan when he says "on the other side of the Jordan." So, who is correct? Both are. When Moses was penning Numbers the Israelites had not yet crossed the Jordan River, so the east side was "this side," the side he was on. On the other hand, when Joshua penned his book, the Israelites had crossed the Jordan, so the east side was just as he had said, "on the other side of the Jordan." Thus, we should not assume that two different writers are writing from the same perspective.

A Careful Reading

At times, it may simply be a case of needing to slow down and carefully read the account, considering exactly what is being said.

Joshua 18:28 Updated American Standard Version (UASV)

²⁸ and Zelah, Haeleph and the Jebusite (that is, Jerusalem), Gibeah, Kiriath; fourteen cities with their villages. This is the inheritance of the sons of Benjamin according to their families.

Judges 1:21 Updated American Standard Version (UASV)

²¹ But the sons of Benjamin did not drive out the Jebusites who lived in Jerusalem; so the Jebusites have lived with the sons of Benjamin in Jerusalem to this day.

Joshua 15:63 Updated American Standard Version (UASV)

⁶³ But as for the Jebusites, the inhabitants of Jerusalem, the sons of Judah could not drive them out; so the Jebusites live with the sons of Judah at Jerusalem until this day.

Judges 1:8-9 Updated American Standard Version (UASV)

⁸And then the sons of Judah fought against Jerusalem and captured it and struck it with the edge of the sword and set the city on fire. ⁹And afterward the sons of Judah went down to fight against the Canaanites living in the hill country and in the Negev[11] and in the Shephelah.[12]

2 Samuel 5:5-9 Updated American Standard Version (UASV)

⁵At Hebron he reigned over Judah seven years and six months, and in Jerusalem he reigned thirty-three years over all Israel and Judah.

⁶And the king and his men went to Jerusalem against the Jebusites, the inhabitants of the land, and they said to David, "You shall not come in here, but the blind and lame will turn you away"; thinking, "David cannot come in here." ⁷Nevertheless, David captured the stronghold of Zion, that is the city of David. ⁸And David said on that day, "Whoever would strike the Jebusites, let him get up the water shaft to attack 'the lame and the blind,' who are hated by David's soul." Therefore it is said, "The blind and the lame shall not come into the house." ⁹And David lived in the stronghold and called it the city of David. And David built all around from the Millo and inward.

There is no doubt that even the advanced Bible reader of many years can come away confused because the above accounts seem to be contradictory. In Joshua 18:28 and Judges 1:21, we see that Jerusalem was an inheritance of the tribe of Benjamin, yet the Benjamites were unable to conquer Jerusalem. However, in Joshua 15:63 we see that the tribe of Judah could not conquer them either, with the reading giving the impression that it was a part of their inheritance. In Judges 1:8, however, Judah was eventually able to conquer Jerusalem and burn it with fire. Yet, to add even more to the confusion, we find at 2 Samuel 5:5–8 that David is said to have conquered Jerusalem hundreds of years later.

Now that we have the particulars let us look at it more clearly. The boundary between Benjamin's inheritances ran right through the middle of Jerusalem. Joshua 8:28 is correct, in that what would later be

---

[11] I.e. *South*

[12] I.e., lowland

called the "city of David" was in the territory of Benjamin, but it also in part crossed over the line into the territory of Judah, causing both tribes to go to war against this Jebusite city. It is also true that the tribe of Benjamin was unable to conquer the city and that the tribe of Judah eventually did. However, if you look at Judges 1:9 again, you will see that Judah did not finish the job entirely and moved on to conquer other areas. This allowed the remaining ones to regroup and form a resistance that neither Benjamin nor Judah could overcome, so these Jebusites remained until the time of David, hundreds of years later.

Intended Meaning of Writer

First, the Bible student needs to understand the level that the Bible intends to be exact in what is written. If Jim told a friend that 650 graduated with him from high school in 1984, it is not challenged, because it is all too clear that he is using rounded numbers and is not meaning to be exactly precise. This is how God's Word operates as well. Sometimes it means to be exact, at other times, it is simply rounding numbers, in other cases, the intention of the writer is a general reference, to give readers of that time and succeeding generations some perspective. Did Samuel, the author of judges, intend to pen a book on the chronology of Judges, or was his focus on the falling away, oppression, and the rescue by a judge, repeatedly. Now, it would seem that Jeremiah, the author of 1 Kings was more interested in giving his readers an exact number of years.

Acts 2:41 Updated American Standard Version (UASV)

[41] So those who received his word were baptized, and there were added that day about three thousand souls.

As you can see here, numbers within the Bible are often used with approximations. This is a frequent practice even today, in both written works and verbal conversation.

Acts 7:2-3 Updated American Standard Version (UASV)

[2] And Stephen said:

"Brothers and fathers, hear me. The God of glory appeared to our father Abraham when he was in Mesopotamia, before he lived in

Haran, ³ and said to him, 'Go out from your land and from your kindred and go into the land that I will show you.'

If you were to check the Hebrew Scriptures at Genesis 12:1, you would find that what is claimed to have been said by God to Abraham is not quoted word-for-word; it is simply a paraphrase. This is a normal practice within Scripture and in writing in general.

Numbers 34:15 Updated American Standard Version (UASV)

¹⁵ The two and a half tribes have received their inheritance beyond the Jordan opposite Jericho, eastward toward the sunrising."

Just as you would read in today's local newspaper, the Bible writer has written from the human standpoint, how it appeared to him. The Bible also speaks of "to the end of the earth" (Psalm 46:9), "from the four corners of the earth" (Isa 11:12), and "the four winds of the earth" (Revelation 7:1). These phrases are still used today.

Unexplained Does Not mean Unexplainable

Considering that there are 31,173 verses in the Bible, encompassing 66 books written by about 40 writers, ranging from shepherds to kings, an army general, fishermen, tax collector, a physician and on and on, and being penned over a 1,600 year period, one does find a few hundred Bible difficulties (about one percent). However, 99 percent of those are explainable. Yet no one wants to be so arrogant to say that he can explain them all. It has nothing to do with the inadequacy of God's Word but is based on human understanding. In many cases, science or archaeology and the field of custom and culture of ancient peoples has helped explain difficulties in hundreds of passages. Therefore, there may be less than one percent left to be answered, yet our knowledge of God's Word continues to grow.

Guilty Until Proven Innocent

This is exactly the perception that the critic has of God's Word. The legal principle of being "innocent until proven guilty" afforded mankind in courts of justice is withheld from the very Word of God. What is ironic here is that this policy has contributed to these Bible critics looking foolish over and over again when something comes to light that vindicates the portion of Scripture they are challenging.

Daniel 5:1 Updated American Standard Version (UASV)

¹ Belshazzar the king made[13] a great feast for a thousand of his nobles, and he was drinking wine in the presence of the thousand.

Bible critics had long claimed that Belshazzar was not known outside of the book Daniel; therefore, they argue that Daniel was mistaken. Yet it hardly seems prudent to argue error from absence of outside evidence. Just because archaeology had not discovered such a person did not mean that Daniel was wrong, or that such a person did not exist. In 1854, some small clay cylinders were discovered in modern-day southern Iraq, which would have been the city of Ur in ancient Babylonia. The cuneiform documents were a prayer of King Nabonidus for "Bel-sar-ussur, my eldest son." These tablets also showed that this "Bel-sar-ussur" had secretaries as well as a household staff. Other tablets were discovered a short time later that showed that the kingship was entrusted to this eldest son as a coregent while his father was away.

He entrusted the 'Camp' to his oldest (son), the firstborn [Belshazzar], the troops everywhere in the country he ordered under his (command). He let (everything) go, entrusted the kingship to him and, himself, he [Nabonidus] started out for a long journey, the (military) forces of Akkad marching with him; he turned towards Tema (deep) in the west."[14]

Ignoring Literary Styles

The Bible is a diverse book when it comes to literary styles: narrative, poetic, prophetic, and apocalyptic; also containing parables, metaphors, similes, hyperbole, and other figures of speech. Too often, these alleged errors are the result of a reader taking a figure of speech as literal, or reading a parable as though it is a narrative.

Matthew 24:35 Updated American Standard Version (UASV)

---

[13] I.e., held

[14] J. Pritchard, ed., *Ancient Near Eastern Texts* (1974), 313.

³⁵ Heaven and earth will pass away, but my words will not pass away.

If some do not recognize that they are dealing with a figure of speech, they are bound to come away with the wrong meaning. Some have concluded from Matthew 24:35 that Jesus was speaking of an eventual destruction of the earth. This is hardly the case, as his listeners would not have understood it that way based on their understanding of the Old Testament. They would have understood that he was simply being emphatic about the words he spoke, using hyperbole. What he was conveying is that his words are more enduring than heaven and earth, and with heaven and earth being understood as eternal, this merely conveyed even more so that Jesus' words could be trusted.

Two Accounts of the Same Incident

If you were to speak to officers that take accident reports for their police department, you would find that there is cohesion in the accounts, but each person has merely witnessed aspects that have stood out to them. We will see that this is the case as well with the examples below, which is the same account in two different gospels:

Matthew 8:5 Updated American Standard Version (UASV)

⁵ When he[15] had entered Capernaum, a centurion came forward to him, imploring him,

Luke 7:2-3 Updated American Standard Version (UASV)

² And a centurion's[16] slave, who was highly regarded[17] by him, was sick and about to die. ³ When he heard about Jesus, he sent some older men of the Jews[18] asking him to come and bring his slave safely through.[19]

Immediately we see the problem of whether the centurion or the elders of the Jews spoke with Jesus. The solution is not really hidden from us. Which of the two accounts is the most detailed account? You

---

[15] That is *Jesus*

[16] I.e., army officer over a hundred solderiers

[17] Lit *to whom he was honorable*

[18] Or *Jewish elders*

[19] I.e., *save the life of his slave*

are correct if you said, Luke. The centurion sent the elders of the Jews to represent him to Jesus, so; that whatever response Jesus might give, it would be as though he were addressing the centurion; therefore, Matthew gave his readers the basic thought, not seeing the need of mentioning the elders of the Jews aspect. This is how a representative was viewed in the first century, just as some countries see ambassadors today as being the very person they represent. Therefore, both Matthew and Luke are correct.

Man's Fallible Interpretations

Inspiration by God is infallible, without error. Imperfect man and his interpretations over the centuries, as bad as many of them have been, should not cast a shadow over God's inspired Word. The entire Word of God has one meaning and one meaning only for every penned word, which is what God willed to be conveyed by the human writer he chose to use.

The Autograph Alone Is Inspired and Inerrant

It has been argued by conservative scholars that only the autograph manuscripts were inspired and inerrant, not the copying of those manuscripts over the next 3,000 years for the Old Testament and 1,500 years for the New Testament. While I would agree with this position as well, it should be noted that we do not possess the autographs, so to argue that they are inerrant is to speak of nonexistent documents. However, it should be further understood that through the science of textual criticism, we can establish a mirror reflection of the autograph manuscripts. B. F. Westcott, F. J. A. Hort, F. F. Bruce, and many other textual scholars would agree with Norman L Geisler's assessment: "The New Testament, then, has not only survived in more manuscripts than any other book from antiquity, but it has survived in a purer form than any other great book—*a form that is 99.5 percent pure.*"[20]

An example of a copyist error can be found in Luke's genealogy of Jesus at Luke 3:35–37. In verse 37 you will find a Cainan, and in verse 36 you will find a second Cainan between Arphaxad

---

[20] Norman L. Geisler and William E. Nix: *A General Introduction to the Bible* (Chicago, Moody Press, 1980), 367. (Emphasis is mine.)

(Arpachshad) and Shelah. As one can see from most footnotes in different study Bibles, the Cainan in verse 36 is seen as a scribal error, and is not found in the Hebrew Old Testament, the Samaritan Pentateuch, or the Aramaic Targums, but is found in the Greek Septuagint. (Genesis 10:24; 11:12, 13; 1 Chronicles 1:18, but not 1 Chronicles 1:24) It seems quite unlikely that it was in the earlier copies of the Septuagint, because the first-century Jewish historian Josephus lists Shelah next as the son of Arphaxad, and Josephus normally followed the Septuagint.[21] So one might ask why this second Cainan is found in the translations at all if this is the case? The manuscripts that do contain this second Cainan are some of the best manuscripts that are used in establishing the original text: 01 B L A^1 33 (Kainam); A 038 044 0102 A^{13} (Kainan).

The Bible Was Miraculously Restored, not Miraculously Preserved

The Hebrew text was like the Greek NT; it had accumulated copyist errors, a few intentional, a good number accidental, between the Malachi days of 440 BCE and Rabbi Judah ha-Nasi (135 to 217 CE). The same thing happened to the Greek New Testament from about 400 CE to 1550 CE, a period of copyist errors. The good news is for the NT is fourfold: (1) the 144 NT papyri discovered in the early part of the 20th century, (2) a number of them dated within decades of the originals, and the great Codex Vaticanus (300-330 CE) and Codex Sinaiticus (330-360 CE), (3) that we have 5,898 Greek NT MSS; (4) then, there was the era of many dozens of textual scholars, from 1550 to the present who restored the text to its original words.

So, the Hebrew OT corruption ran in earnest between 440 BCE to 220 CE. At that time, the Greek Septuagint, a translation of the Hebrew Scriptures, was produced between 280 – 150 BCE, which became favored by the Jews to the point that they claimed it was inspired. However, the fact that the lingua franca of the Roman Empire ran from 330 BCE to 330 CE, the Christians in the first century CE wisely used the Greek Septuagint to evangelize, to show that Jesus Christ was the long-awaited Messiah. Then, Jerusalem was

---

[21] *Jewish Antiquities,* I, 146 [vi, 4].

destroyed by General Titus and the Roman army in 70 CE, killing one million one hundred thousand Jews and carrying another seventy thousand back to Rome as slaves. No temple led to the creation of the Mishnah, an authoritative collection of exegetical material embodying the oral tradition of Jewish law and forming the first part of the Talmud. During the 150 years in the wake of the temple's destruction in Jerusalem in 70 CE, rabbinic sages throughout Israel at once were quick to seek out a new source for preserving Jewish practice. They debated and combined various traditions of their oral law. Growing this foundation, they set new constraints, boundaries, and requirements for Judaism. This gave the Jewish people direction for their day-to-day life of holiness, even though they lacked a temple. This new spiritual structure was summarized in the Mishnah, which Judah ha-Nasi compiled by about 200-217 CE.

In addition, the Jewish scholars set about creating a corrected text of the Hebrew Old Testament because they realized it had some textual variants from the sopherim (scribes). But it was the greatest textual scholars who have ever lived, the Masoretes, who made corrected copies from 500 to 900 CE. Below is an article about them. The beauty is that they did not erase the manuscripts with the errors; they kept them, then simply put the corrections in the margin, called the Masorah. So, the Hebrew text was corrected just as the Greek text was. And then, in 1947, we found the Dead Sea Scrolls, which dated as early as the 3rd century BCE and validated the Masoretic text. And ironically at this same time, many of the **best** NT papyri were coming to light that validated the work of Johann Jakob Wettstein [1693-1754 A.D.], Karl Lachmann [1793-1851], Samuel Prideaux Tregelles [1813-1875], Friedrich Constantin von Tischendorf [1815-1874], and especially Westcott and Hort of 1881.

MIRACULOUS RESTORATION, NOT MIRACULOUS PRESERVATION

OLD TESTAMENT
Transmission: 1500 BCE – 440 BCE
Corruption: 440 BCE – 220 CE
Restoration: 500 – 900 CE – Present
Corroboration MSS (Dead Sea Scrolls): 1947

NEW TESTAMENT
Transmission: 45 CE – 98 CE
Corruption: 440 CE -1550 CE
Restoration: 1550 CE – Present
Corroboration MSS (NT Papyri): 1900s-1960s-Present

A Lack of <u>Preservation</u> Does Not Mean a Lack of <u>Inspiration</u>

- The Bible **was miraculously inspired** as men were moved along by the Holy Spirit (*Absolute Inerrancy*)

- The Bible **was not miraculously preserved** as men's human imperfection gave us corruption (*Limited Inerrancy*)

- The Bible **was restored** through tens of millions of hours by many hundreds of (men) textual scholars from the 16th to the 21st centuries. (*Absolute Inerrancy Restored*)

The **men who restored the text** are no more perfect than the **men who** intentionally and unintentionally **corrupted the text**. However, even hundreds of **imperfect men**, through dozens of lifetimes of sweat and toil, arrived at **a perfect text** that was lost but now is found. With the copyists, you have tens of thousands of men **focusing on their work as an individual** in reproducing a copy; with the textual scholars, it is teams of hundreds of men focusing on all of the manuscripts to ascertain the original words of the original texts.

Many of the above scholars gave their entire lives to God and the Hebrew and Greek text.[22] Each of these could have an entire book

---

[22] The Climax of the Restored Text

devoted to them and their work alone. The amount of work they accomplished before the era of computers is nothing short of astonishing. Rightly, the preceding history should serve to strengthen our faith in the authenticity and general integrity of the Hebrew Scriptures and the Greek New Testament. Unlike Bart D. Ehrman, men like Sir Frederic Kenyon have been moved to say that the books of the Greek New Testament have "come down to us substantially as they were written." And all this is especially true of the critical scholarship of the almost two hundred years since the days of Karl Lachmann. All today can feel confident that what they hold in their hands is a mirror reflection of the Word of God that was penned in twenty-seven books, some two thousand years ago.

It is true that the Jewish copyists and the later Christian copyists were not led along by the Holy Spirit, and therefore their manuscripts were not inerrant, infallible. Errors (textual variants) crept into the manuscripts unintentionally and intentionally. However, the vast majority of the Hebrew Old Testament and Greek New Testament has not been infected with textual errors. For the portions impacted with textual errors, it is the many tens of thousands of copies that we have to help us to weed out the errors. How? Well, not every copyist made the same textual errors. Hence, by comparing the work of different copyists and different manuscripts, textual scholars can identify the textual variants (errors) and remove those, leaving us with the original content.

Yes, it would be the greatest discovery of all time if we found the actual original five books that were penned by Moses himself, Genesis through Deuteronomy. However, there would be no way of establishing that they were the originals. The fact is, we do not need the originals. We do not need those original documents. What is so important about the documents? The documents are not important; it is the content on the original documents that we are after. And truly, miraculously, we have more copies than needed to do just that. We do not need miraculous preservation because we have miraculous restoration. We now know beyond a reasonable doubt that the Hebrew Old Testament and the Greek New Testament critical texts are a 99.99% reflection of the content that was in those ancient original manuscripts. Some textual scholars might say that I am exaggerating with the 99.99%. An example of how that is not so can be found in the 1881 Westcott and Hort critical Greek NT, which is 99.5% the same as the 2012 28th edition of the critical Greek NT. The discovery of the NT papyri from the 1900s to the 1960s and up to the present has validated Westcott and Hort's Greek NT and let us know that the 2012 Nestle-Aland Greek NT is a mirror-like reflection of the original. To be frank, there are about 100+ textual variants where Westcott and Hort were correct, and the Nestle-Aland text is likely not correct. This is because they took the textual eclecticism method of determining the original, which was to focus on both external and internal evidence. Still, they leaned heavily on internal evidence, which is a bit more subjective. Regardless, we have the apparatus in the 28th edition of the Nestle-Aland that gives the translator the variants, allowing him to make an objective determination. Therefore, the 100+ textual variants can be decided on a case-by-case basis. So, yes, what we have is 99.99% reflective of the original.

The critical text of Westcott and Hort of 1881 [(FENTON JOHN ANTHONY HORT (1828 – 1892) and BROOKE FOSS WESTCOTT (1825 – 1901)] has been commended by leading textual scholars over the last one hundred and forty years, and still stands as the standard. Numerous additional critical editions of the Greek text came after Westcott and Hort: Richard F. Weymouth (1886), Bernhard Weiss (1894–1900); the British and Foreign Bible Society (1904, 1958), Alexander Souter (1910), Hermann von Soden (1911–1913); and Eberhard Nestle's Greek text, *Novum Testamentum Graece*, published in 1898 by the Württemberg Bible Society, Stuttgart, Germany. The Nestle in twelve editions (1898–1923) to subsequently be taken over by his son, Erwin Nestle (13th–20th editions, 1927–1950), followed by Kurt Aland (21st–25th editions, 1952–1963), and lastly, it was coedited by Kurt Aland and Barbara Aland (26th–28th editions, 1979, 1993, 2012).

Look at the Context

Many alleged inconsistencies disappear by simply looking at the context. Taking words out of context can distort their meaning. *Merriam-Webster's Collegiate Dictionary* defines context as "the parts of a discourse that surround a word or passage and can throw light on its meaning."²³ Context can also be "the circumstances or events that form the environment within which something exists or takes place." If we were to look in a thesaurus for a synonym, we would find "background" for this second meaning. At 2 Timothy 2:15, the apostle Paul brings home the point of why context is so important: "Do your best to present yourself to God as one approved, a worker who has no need to be ashamed, rightly handling the word of truth."

Ephesians 2:8-9 Updated American Standard Version (UASV)

⁸ For by grace you have been saved through faith; and that not of yourselves, it is the gift of God; ⁹ not from works, so that no man may boast.

James 2:26 Updated American Standard Version (UASV)

²⁶ For as the body apart from the spirit²⁴ is dead, so also faith apart from works is dead.

So, which is it? Is salvation possible by faith alone as Paul wrote to the Ephesians, or is faith dead without works as James wrote to his readers? As our subtitle brings out, let us look at the context. In the letter to the Ephesians, the apostle Paul is speaking to the Jewish Christians who were looking to the works of the Mosaic Law as a means to salvation, a righteous standing before God. Paul was telling these legalistic Jewish Christians that this is not so. In fact, this would invalidate Christ's ransom because there would have been no need for it if one could achieve salvation by meticulously keeping the Mosaic Law. (Rom. 5:18) But James was writing to those in a congregation who were concerned with their status before other men, who were looking for prominent positions within the congregation, and not taking care of those that were in need. (Jam. 2:14–17) So, James is merely addressing those who call themselves Christian, but in name only. No person could truly be a Christian and not possess some good works, such as feeding the poor, helping the elderly. This type of work was an evident demonstration of one's Christian personality. Paul was in perfect harmony with James on this. – Romans 10:10; 1 Corinthians

---

²³ Merriam-Webster, Inc: *Merriam-Webster's Collegiate Dictionary*. Eleventh ed. (Springfield, Mass.: Merriam-Webster, Inc. 2003).

²⁴ Or *breath*

15:58; Ephesians 5:15, 21–33; 6:15; 1 Timothy 4:16; 2 Timothy 4:5; Hebrews 10:23-25.

Inerrancy: Are There Contradictions?

Below I will follow this pattern. I will list the critic's argument first, followed by the text of difficulty, and conclude with an answer to the critic. What should be kept at the forefront of our mind is this: one is simply looking for the best answer, not absoluteness. If there is a reasonable answer to a Bible difficulty, why are the critics able to set them aside with ease? Because they start with the premise that this is not the Word of God, but only a book by imperfect men and full of contradictions; thus, the bias toward errors has blinded their judgment.

Critic: The critic would argue that there was an Adam and Eve, and an Abel who was now dead, so, where did Cain get his wife? This is one of the most common questions by Bible critics.

Genesis 4:17 Updated American Standard Version (UASV)

¹⁷ Cain had sexual relations[25] with his wife and she conceived, and gave birth to Enoch; and he built a city, and called the name of the city Enoch, after the name of his son, Enoch.

Answer: If one were to read a little further along, they would come to the realization that Adam had a son named Seth; it further adds that Adam "became father to sons *and daughters*." (Genesis 5:4) Adam lived for a total of 800 years after fathering Seth, giving him ample opportunity to father many more sons and daughters. So it could be that Cain married one of his sisters. If he waited until one of his brothers and sisters had a daughter, he could have married one of his nieces once she was old enough. In the beginning, humans were closer to perfection; this explains why they lived longer and why at that time there was little health risk of genetic defects in the case of children born to closely related parents, in contrast to how it is today. As time passed, genetic defects increased and life spans decreased. Adam lived to see 930 years. Yet Shem, who lived after the Flood, died at 600 years, while Shem's son Arpachshad only lived 438 years, dying before his father died. Abraham saw an even greater decrease in that he only lived

---

[25] Lit *knew*

175 years while his grandson Jacob was 147 years when he died. Thus, due to increasing imperfection, God prohibited the marriage of closely related people under the Mosaic Law because of the likelihood of genetic defects.—Leviticus 18:9.

Critic: If God is here hardening Pharaoh's heart, what exactly makes Pharaoh responsible for the decisions he makes?

Exodus 4:21 Updated American Standard Version (UASV)

²¹ Jehovah said to Moses, "When you go and return to Egypt see that you perform before Pharaoh all the wonders which I have put in your hand; but I will harden his heart so that he will not let the people go.

Answer: This is actually a prophecy. God knew that what he was about to do would contribute to a stubborn and obstinate Pharaoh, who was going to be unwilling to change or give up the Israelites so they could go off to worship their God. Therefore, this is not stating what God is going to do; it is prophesying that Pharaoh's heart will harden because of the actions of God. The fact is, Pharaoh allowed his own heart to harden because he was determined not to agree with Moses' wishes or accept Jehovah's request to let the people go. Moses tells us at Exodus 7:13 (ESV) that "Pharaoh's heart was hardened, and he would not listen to them, as the Lord had said." Again, at 8:15 we read, "When Pharaoh saw that there was a respite, he hardened his heart and would not listen to them, as the Lord had said."

Critic: The Israelites had just received the Ten Commandments, with one commandment being: "You shall not make for yourself a carved image or any likeness of anything that is in heaven above, or that is in the earth beneath, or that is in the water under the earth." Therefore, how is the bronze serpent not a violation of this commandment?

Numbers 21:9 Updated American Standard Version (UASV)

⁹ And Moses made a bronze serpent and set it on the standard;²⁶ and it came about, that if a serpent bit any man, when he looked to the bronze serpent, he lived.

Answer: First, an idol is "a representation or symbol of an object of worship; *broadly*: a false god."²⁷ Second, it should be noted that not all images are idols. The bronze serpent was not made for the purpose of worship, or for some passionate devotion or veneration. There were times, however, when images were created with absolutely no intention of it receiving devotion, veneration, or worship, yet were later made into objects of veneration. That is exactly what happened with the copper serpent that Moses had formed in the wilderness. Many centuries later, "in the third year of Hoshea son of Elah, king of Israel, Hezekiah the son of Ahaz, king of Judah, began to reign. He removed the high places and broke the pillars and cut down the Asherah. And he broke in pieces the bronze serpent that Moses had made; for until those days the people of Israel had made offerings to it (it was called Nehushtan)."—2 Kings 18:1, 4.

Critic: Deuteronomy 15:11 (NET) says: *"There will never cease to be some poor people in the land;* therefore, I am commanding you to make sure you open your hand to your fellow Israelites who are needy and poor in your land." Is this not a contradiction of Deuteronomy 15:4? Will there be no poor among the Israelites, or will there be poor among them? Which is it?

Deuteronomy 15:4 Updated American Standard Version (UASV)

⁴ However, there will be no poor among you, since Jehovah will surely bless you in the land which Jehovah your God is giving you as an inheritance to possess,

Answer: If you look at the context, Deuteronomy 15:4 is stating that if the Israelites obey Jehovah's command to take care of the poor, "there should not be any poor among" them. Thus, for every poor person, there will be one to take care of that need. If an Israelite fell

---

²⁶ I.e., *pole*

²⁷ Merriam-Webster, Inc: *Merriam-Webster's Collegiate Dictionary*. Eleventh ed. (Springfield, Mass.: Merriam-Webster, Inc., 2003).

on hard times, there was to be a fellow Israelite ready to step in to help him through those hard times. Verse 11 stresses the truth of the imperfect world since the rebellion of Adam and inherited sin: there will always be poor among mankind, the Israelites being no different. However, the difference with God's people is that those who were well off financially were to offset conditions for those who fell on difficult times. This is not to be confused with the socialistic welfare systems in the world today. Those Jews were hard-working men, who labored from sunup to sundown to take care of their families. But if disease overtook their herd or unseasonal weather brought about failed crops, an Israelite could sell himself into the service of a fellow Israelite for a period of time; thereafter, he would be back on his feet. And many years down the road, he may very well do the same for another Israelite, who fell on difficult times.

Critic: Joshua 11:23 says that Joshua took the land according to what God had spoken to Moses and handed it on to the nation of Israel as planned. However, in Joshua 13:1, God is telling Joshua that he has grown old and much of the Promised Land has yet to be taken possession of. How can both be true? Is this not a contradiction?

Joshua 11:23 Updated American Standard Version (UASV)

²³ So Joshua took the whole land, according to all that Jehovah had spoken to Moses, and Joshua gave it for an inheritance to Israel according to their divisions by their tribes, and the land had rest from war.

Joshua 13:1 Updated American Standard Version (UASV)

13 Now Joshua was old and advanced in years, and Jehovah said to him, "You are old and advanced in years, and there remains yet very much land to possess.

Answer: No, it is not a contradiction. When the Israelites were to take the land, it was to take place in two different stages: the nation as a whole was to go to war and defeat the 31 kings of this land; thereafter, each Israelite tribe was to take their part of the land based on their individual actions. (Joshua 17:14–18; 18:3) Joshua fulfilled his role, which is expressed in 11:23 while the individual tribes did not complete their campaigns, which is expressed in 13:1. Even though the individual tribes failed to live up to taking their portion, the remaining Canaanites posed no real threat. Joshua 21:44, *ASV,* reads: "Jehovah gave them rest round about."

Critic: The critic would point out that John 1:18 clearly says that "*no one has ever seen God*," while Exodus 24:10 explicitly states that Moses and Aaron, Nadab and Abihu, and seventy of the elders of Israel "*saw the God of Israel.*" Worse still, God informs them in Exodus 33:20: "You cannot see my face, for man shall not see me and live." The critic with his knowing smile says, 'This is a blatant contradiction.'

John 1:18 Updated American Standard Version (UASV)

[18] No one has seen God at any time; the only begotten god[28] who is in the bosom of the Father,[29] that one has made him fully known.

Exodus 24:10 Updated American Standard Version (UASV)

[10] and they saw the God of Israel; and under his feet was what seemed like a sapphire pavement, as clear as the sky itself.

Exodus 33:20 Updated American Standard Version (UASV)

[20] But he [God] said, "You cannot see my face, for no man can see me and live!"

Answer: Exodus 33:20 is one-hundred percent correct: No human could see Jehovah God and live. The apostle Paul at Colossians 1:15 tell us that Christ is the image of the invisible God, and the writer informs us at Hebrews 1:3 that Jesus is the "exact representation of His nature." Yet if you were to read the account of Saul of Tarsus (the apostle Paul), you would see that a mere partial manifestation of Christ's glory blinded Saul – Acts 9:1–18.

When the Bible says that Moses and others have seen God, it is not speaking of *literally* seeing him, because first of all He is an invisible spirit person. It is a *manifestation* of his glory, which is an act of showing or demonstrating his presence, making himself perceptible to the human mind. In fact, it is generally an angelic representative that stands

---

[28] Jn 1:18: "only-begotten god", P⁶⁶ℵ*BC*Lsyr^hmg,p; **[V1]** "the only-begotten god," P⁷⁵33ℵcop^bo; **[V2]** "the only-begotten Son." AC³(W^s)QYf1,13 MajVgSyr^c

[29] Or *at the Father's side*

in his place and not him personally. Exodus 24:16 informs us that "the glory of the Lord dwelt on Mount Sinai," not the Lord himself personally. When texts such as Exodus 24:10 explicitly state that Moses and Aaron, Nadab and Abihu, and seventy of the elders of Israel "*saw the God of Israel*," it is this "glory of the Lord," an angelic representative. This is shown to be the case at Luke 2:9, which reads: "And *an angel of the Lord* appeared to them, and *the glory of the Lord shone around them* [the shepherds], and they were filled with fear."

Many Bible difficulties are cleared up elsewhere in Scripture; for example, in the New Testament, you will find a text clarifying a difficulty from the Old Testament, such as Acts 7:53, which refers to those "who received the law *as delivered by angels* and did not keep it." Support comes from Paul at Galatians 3:19: "Why then the law? It was added because of transgressions until the offspring should come to whom the promise had been made, and it was put in place through angels by an intermediary." The writer of Hebrews chimes in at 2:2 with "For since the message *declared by angels* proved to be reliable, and every transgression or disobedience received a just retribution. . . ." As we travel back to Exodus again, to 19:19 specifically, we find support that it was not God's own voice, which Moses heard; no, it was an angelic representative, for it reads: "Moses was speaking, and God was answering him with a voice." Exodus 33:22–23 also helps us to appreciate that it was the back of these angelic representatives of Jehovah that Moses saw: "While my glory passes by . . . Then I will take away my hand, and you shall see my back, but my face shall not be seen."

Exodus 3:4 states: "God called to him out of the bush, 'Moses, Moses!' And he said, 'Here I am.'" Verse 6 informs us: "I am the God of your father, the God of Abraham, the God of Isaac, and the God of Jacob." Yet, in verse 2 we read: "And the angel of the Lord appeared to him in a flame of fire out of the midst of a bush." Here is another example of using God's Word to clear up what seems to be unclear or difficult to understand at first glance. Thus, while it speaks of the Lord making a direct appearance, it is really an angelic representative. Even today, we hear such comments, as 'the president of the United States is to visit the Middle East later this week.' However, later in the article it is made clear that he is not going personally, but it is one of his high-ranking representatives. Let us close with two examples, starting with,

Genesis 32:24-30 Updated American Standard Version (UASV)

^{24} And Jacob was left alone, and a man wrestled with him until daybreak. ^{25} When he saw that he had not prevailed against him, he touched the socket of his thigh; so the socket of Jacob's thigh was dislocated as he wrestled with him. ^{26} Then he said, "Let me go, for the dawn is breaking." But he said, "I will not let you go unless you bless me." ^{27} And he said to him, "What is your name?" And he said, "Jacob." ^{28} And he said, "Your name shall no longer be called Jacob, but Israel,^{30} for you have struggled with God and with men and have prevailed." ^{29} Then Jacob asked him and said, "Please tell me your name." But he said, "Why is it that you ask my name?" And he blessed him there. ^{30} So Jacob named the place Peniel,^{31} for he said, "I have seen God face to face, yet my soul has been preserved."

It is all too obvious here that this man is simply a materialized angel in the form of a man, another angelic representative of Jehovah God. Moreover, the reader of this book should have taken in that the Israelites as a whole saw these angelic representatives and spoke of them as though they were dealing directly with Jehovah God himself.

This proved to be the case in the second example found in the book of Judges where an angelic representative visited Manoah and his wife. Like the above mentioned account, Manoah and his wife treated this angelic representative as if he were Jehovah God himself: "And Manoah said to the angel of the Lord, 'What is your name, so that, when your words come true, we may honor you?' And the angel of the Lord said to him, 'Why do you ask my name, seeing it is wonderful?' Then Manoah knew that he was the angel of the Lord. And Manoah said to his wife, "We shall surely die, *for we have seen God*." – Judges 13:3–22.

---

[30] Meaning *he contends with God*

[31] Meaning *face of God*

IS THE BIBLE REALLY THE WORD OF GOD?

Inerrancy: Are There Mistakes?

I have addressed the alleged contradictions, so it would seem that our job is done here, right? Not hardly. Yes, there are just as many who claim that the Bible is full of mistakes.

Critic: Matthew 27:5 states that Judas hanged himself, whereas Acts 1:18 says, "Falling headlong, he burst open in the middle and all his intestines gushed out."

Matthew 27:5 Updated American Standard Version (UASV)

⁵ And he threw the pieces of silver into the temple and departed; and he went away and hanged himself.

Acts 1:18 Updated American Standard Version (UASV)

¹⁸ (Now this man acquired a field with the price of his wickedness, and falling headlong, he burst open in the middle and all his intestines gushed out.

Answer: Neither Matthew nor Luke made a mistake. What you have is Matthew giving the reader the manner in which Judas committed suicide. On the other hand, Luke is giving the reader of Acts, the result of that suicide. Therefore, instead of a mistake, we have two texts that complement each other, really giving the reader the full picture. Judas came to a tree alongside a cliff that had rocks below. He tied the rope to a branch and the other end around his neck and jumped over the edge of the cliff in an attempt at hanging himself. One of two things could have happened: (1) the limb broke plunging him to the rocks below, or (2) the rope broke with the same result, and he burst open onto the rocks below.

Critic: The apostle Paul made a mistake when he quotes how many people died.

Numbers 25:9 Updated American Standard Version (UASV)

⁹ The ones who died in the plague were twenty-four thousand.

1 Corinthians 10:8 Updated American Standard Version (UASV)

⁸ Neither let us commit sexual immorality, as some of them committed sexual immorality, only to fall, twenty-three thousand of them in one day.

Answer: We must keep in mind the above principle that we spoke of, the *Intended Meaning of the Writer*. We live in a far more precise age today, where specificity is highly important. However, we round large numbers off (even estimate) all the time: "there were 237,000 people in Time Square last night." The simplest answer is that the number of people slain was in between 23,000 and 24,000, and both writers rounded the number off. However, there is even another possibility, because the book of Numbers specifically speaks of "all the chiefs of the people" (25:4-5), which could account for the extra 1,000, which is mentioned in Numbers 24,000. Thus, you have the people killing the chiefs of the people and the plague killing the people. Therefore, both books are correct.

Critic: After 215 years in Egypt, the descendants of Jacob arrived at the Promised Land. As you recall they sinned against God and were sentenced to forty years in the wilderness. But once they entered the Promised Land, they buried Joseph's bones "at Shechem, in the piece of land that *Jacob bought* from the sons of Hamor the father of Shechem," as stated at Joshua 24:32. Yet, when Stephen had to defend himself before the Jewish religious leaders, he said that Joseph was buried "in the tomb that *Abraham had bought* for a sum of silver from the sons of Hamor." Therefore, at once it appears that we have a mistake on the part of Stephen.

Acts 7:15-16 Updated American Standard Version (UASV)

¹⁵ And Jacob went down to Egypt and died, he and our fathers. ¹⁶ And they were brought back to Shechem and buried in the tomb that Abraham had bought for a sum of silver from the sons of Hamor in Shechem.

Genesis 23:17-18 Updated American Standard Version (UASV)

¹⁷ So Ephron's field, which was in Machpelah, which faced Mamre, the field and cave which was in it, and all the trees which were in the field, that were in all its border around, were made over ¹⁸ to Abraham

for a possession in the presence of the sons of Heth, before all who went in at the gate of his city.

Genesis 33:19 Updated American Standard Version (UASV)

¹⁹ And he bought the piece of land where he had pitched his tent from the hand of the sons of Hamor, Shechem's father, for one hundred qesitahs.³²

Joshua 24:32 Updated American Standard Version (UASV)

³² As for the bones of Joseph, which the sons of Israel brought up from Egypt, they buried them at Shechem, in the piece of land that Jacob bought from the sons of Hamor the father of Shechem for one hundred qesitahs.³³ It became an inheritance of the sons of Joseph.

Answer: If we look back to Genesis 12:6-7, we will find that Abraham's first stop after entering Canaan from Haran was Shechem. It is here that Jehovah told Abraham: "To your offspring I will give this land." At this point Abraham built an altar to Jehovah. It seems reasonable that Abraham would need to purchase this land that had not yet been given to his offspring. While it is true that the Old Testament does not mention this purchase, it is likely that Stephen would be aware of such by way of oral tradition. As Acts chapter seven demonstrates, Stephen had a wide-ranging knowledge of Old Testament history.

Later, Jacob would have had difficulty laying claim to the tract of land that his grandfather Abraham had purchased, because there would have been a new generation of inhabitants of Shechem. This would have been many years after Abraham moved further south and Isaac moved to Beersheba, and including Jacob's twenty years in Paddan-aram (Gen 28:6, 7). The simplest answer is that this land was not in use for about 120 years because of Abraham's extensive travels and Isaac's having moved away, leaving it unused; likely it was put to use by others. So, Jacob simply repurchased what Abraham had bought over a hundred years earlier. This is very similar to the time Isaac had

---

³² Or *pieces of money*; money of unknown value
³³ Or *pieces of money*; money of unknown value

to repurchase the well at Beersheba that Abraham had already purchased earlier. – Genesis 21:27–30; 26:26–32.

Genesis 33:18–20 tells us that 'Jacob bought this land for a hundred pieces of money, from the sons of Hamor.' This same transaction is also mentioned at Joshua 24:32, in reference to transporting Joseph's bones from Egypt, to be buried in Shechem.

We should also address the cave of Machpelah that Abraham had purchased in Hebron from Ephron the Hittite. The word "tomb" is not mentioned until Joshua 24:32, and is in reference to the tract of land in Shechem. Nowhere in the Old Testament does it say that Abraham bought a "tomb." The cave of Machpelah obtained by Abraham would eventually become a family tomb, receiving Sarah's body and, eventually, his own, and those of Isaac, Rebekah, Jacob, and Leah. (Genesis 23:14–19; 25:9; 49:30, 31; 50:13) Gleason L. Archer, Jr., concludes this Bible difficulty, saying:

> The reference to a *mnema* ("tomb") in connection with Shechem must either have been proleptic [to anticipate] for the later use of that shechemite tract for Joseph's tomb (i.e., 'the tomb that Abraham bought' was intended to imply 'the tomb location that Abraham bought"); or else conceivably the dative relative pronoun *ho* was intended elliptically [omission] for *en to topo ho onesato Abraam* ("in the place that Abraham bought") as describing the location of the *mnema* near the Oak of Moreh right outside Shechem. Normally Greek would have used the relative-locative adverb *hou* to express 'in which' or 'where'; but this would have left o*nesato* ("bought") without an object in its own clause, and so *ho* was much more suitable in this context. (Archer 1982, 379–81)

Another solution could be that Jacob is being viewed as a representative of Abraham, for he is the grandson of Abraham. This was quite appropriate in Biblical times, to attribute the purchase to Abraham as the Patriarchal family head.

Critic: 2 Samuel 24:1 says that God moved David to count the Israelites, while 1 Chronicles 21:1 Satan, or a resister did. This would seem to be a clear mistake on the part of one of these authors.

IS THE BIBLE REALLY THE WORD OF GOD?

2 Samuel 24:1 Updated American Standard Version (UASV)

¹ Now again the anger of Jehovah burned against Israel, and it incited David against them to say, "Go, number Israel and Judah."

1 Chronicles 21:1 Updated American Standard Version (UASV)

¹ Then Satan stood up against Israel and moved David to number Israel.

Answer: In this period of David's reign, Jehovah was very displeased with Israel, and therefore he did not prevent Satan from bringing this sin on them. Often in Scripture, it is spoken of as though God did something when he allowed an event to take place. For example, it is said that God 'hardened Pharaoh's heart' (Exodus 4:21), when he actually allowed the Pharaoh's heart to harden.

Inerrancy: Are There Scientific Errors?

Many truths about God are beyond the scope of science. Science and the Bible are not at odds. In fact, we can thank modern day science as it has helped us to better under the creation of God, from our solar system to the universes, to the human body and mind. What we find is a level of order, precision, design, and sophistication, which points to a Designer, the eyes of many Christians, to an Almighty God, with infinite intelligence and power. The apostle Paul makes this all too clear, when he writes, "For his invisible attributes, namely, his eternal power and divine nature, have been clearly perceived, ever since the creation of the world, in the things that have been made. So they are without excuse." – Romans 1:20.

Back in the seventeenth century, the world-renowned scientist Galileo proved beyond any doubt that the earth was not the center of the universe, nor did the sun orbit the earth. In fact, he proved it to be the other way around (no pun intended), with the earth revolving around the sun. However, he was brought up on charges of heresy by the Catholic Church and ordered to recant his position. Why? From the viewpoint of the Catholic Church, Galileo was contradicting God's Word, the Bible. As it turned out, Galileo and science were correct, and the Church was wrong, for which it issued a formal apology in 1992. However, the point we wish to make here is that in all the controversy, the Bible was never in the wrong. It was a misinterpretation on the part of the Catholic Church and not a fault with the Bible. One will find no place in the Bible that claims the sun orbits the earth. So where would the Church get such an idea? The Church got such an idea from Ptolemy (b. about 85 C.E.), an ancient astronomer, who argued for such an idea.

As it usually turns out, the so-called contradiction between science and God's Word lies at the feet of those who are interpreting Scripture incorrectly. To repeat the sentiments of Galileo when writing to a pupil—Galileo expressed the same sentiments: "Even though Scripture cannot err, its interpreters and expositors can, in various ways. One of these, very serious and very frequent, would be when they always want to stop at the purely literal sense."[34] I believe that today's scholars, in hindsight, would have no problem agreeing.

While the Bible is not a science textbook, it is scientifically accurate when it touches on matters of science.

The Circle of the Earth Hangs on Nothing

Isaiah 40:22 Updated American Standard Version (UASV)

[22] It is he who sits above **the circle of the earth**,
   and its inhabitants are like grasshoppers;
who stretches out the heavens like a curtain,
   and spreads them like a tent to dwell in.

More than 2,500 years ago, the prophet Isaiah wrote that the earth is a circle or sphere. First, how would it be possible for Isaiah to know the earth is a circle or sphere, if not from inspiration? Scientific America writes, "As countless photos from space can attest, Earth is round—the "Blue Marble," as astronauts have affectionately dubbed it. Appearances, however, can be deceiving. Planet Earth is not, in fact, perfectly round."[35] Scientifically speaking, the sun is not perfectly, absolutely 100 percent round but in everyday speech, this verse is both

---

[34] Letter from Galileo to Benedetto Castelli, December 21, 1613.

[35] Charles Q. Choi (April 12, 2007). Scientific America. Strange but True: Earth Is Not Round. Retrieved Monday, August 03, 2015.

http://www.scientificamerican.com/article/earth-is-not-round/

acceptable and accurate, when we keep in mind it is written from a human perspective, not from a scientific perspective. Moreover, Isaiah was not discussing astronomy; he was simply making an inspired observation that man came to realize once he was in space, looking back at the earth, it is round. See the section about title, "Intended Meaning of Writer."

Job 26:7 Updated American Standard Version (UASV)

⁷ "He stretches out the north over empty space
and hangs the earth on nothing.

Here the author describes the earth as hanging upon nothing. Many have never heard of the Greek mathematician and astronomer Eratosthenes. He was born in about 276 B.C.E. and received some of his education in Athens, Greece. In 240 B.C., the "Greek astronomer, geographer, mathematician and librarian Eratosthenes calculates the Earth's circumference. His data was rough, but he wasn't far off."[36] While man very early on used their God given intelligence to arrive at some outstanding conclusion that was actually very accurate, we learn two points here. Eratosthenes was a very astute scientist, while Isaiah, who wrote some 500 years earlier, was no scientist at all. Moreover, Moses, who wrote the book of Job over 1,230 years before Eratosthenes, knew that the earth hung upon nothing.

How Is the Sun Standing Still Possible?

Joshua 10:13 Updated American Standard Version (UASV)

¹³ And the sun stood still, and the moon stopped,
until the nation avenged themselves of their enemies.

Is this not written in the Book of Jashar? The sun stopped in the midst of heaven and did not hurry to set for about a whole day.

The Canaanites had besieged the Gibeonites, a group of people that gained Jehovah God's backing because they had faith in Him. In this battle, Jehovah helped the Israelites continue their attack by causing "the sun [to stand] still, and the moon stopped, until the nation

---

[36] Alfred, Randy (June 19, 2008). "June 19, 240 B.C.E: The Earth Is Round, and It's This Big". Wired. Retrieved Monday, August 03, 2015.

took vengeance on their enemies." (Jos 10:1-14) Those who accept God as the creator of the universe and life can accept that he would know a way of stopping the earth from rotating. However, there are other ways of understanding this account. We must keep in mind that the Bible speaks from an earthly observer point of view, so it need not be that he stopped the rotation. It could have been a refraction of solar and lunar light rays, which would have produced the same effect.

Psalm 136:6 Updated American Standard Version (UASV)

⁶ to him who spread out the earth above the waters,

    for his lovingkindness is everlasting;

Hebrews 3:4 Updated American Standard Version (UASV)

⁴ For every house is built by someone, but the builder of all things is God.

2 Kings 20:8-11 Updated American Standard Version (UASV)

⁸ And Hezekiah said to Isaiah, "What shall be the sign that Jehovah will heal me, and that I shall go up to the house of Jehovah on the third day?" ⁹ And Isaiah said, "This shall be the sign to you from Jehovah, that Jehovah will do the thing that he has spoken: shall the shadow go forward ten steps or go back ten steps?" ¹⁰ And Hezekiah answered, "It is an easy thing for the shadow to decline ten steps; no, but let the shadow turn backward ten steps." ¹¹ And Isaiah the prophet cried to Jehovah, and he brought the shadow on the steps back ten steps, by which it had gone down on the steps of Ahaz.

How is it that the stars fought on behalf of Barak?

Judges 5:20 Updated American Standard Version (UASV)

²⁰ From heaven the stars fought, from their courses they fought against Sisera.

Judges 4:15 Updated American Standard Version (UASV)

¹⁵ And Jehovah routed Sisera and all his chariots and all his army with the edge of the sword before Barak; and Sisera alighted from his chariot and fled away on foot.

In the Bible, you have Biblical prose, and Biblical poetry.

IS THE BIBLE REALLY THE WORD OF GOD?

Prose: language that is not poetry: (1) writing or speech in its normal continuous form, without the rhythmic or visual line structure of poetry **(2)** ordinary style of expression: writing or speech that is ordinary or matter-of-fact, without embellishment.

Poetry: literature in verse: (1) literary works written in verse, in particular verse writing of high quality, great beauty, emotional sincerity or intensity, or profound insight **(2) beauty or grace:** something that resembles poetry in its beauty, rhythmic grace, or imaginative, elevated, or decorative style.

We have a beautiful example of both of these forms of writing communication in chapters four and five of the book of Judges. Judges, Chapter 4 is a prose account of Deborah and Barak, while Judges Chapter 5 is a poetic account. As we have learned from the above, poetry is less concerned with accuracy than evoking emotions. Poetry has a license to say things like what we find in of 5:20, which is in the poetry chapter: "from heaven the stars fought." This can be said, and the reader is expected not to take the language literally. What we can surmise from it though, is that God was acting against Sisera in some way, there was divine intervention.

Procedures for Handling Biblical Difficulties

1. You need to be completely convinced a reason or understanding exists.

2. You need to have total trust and conviction in the inerrancy of the Scripture as originally written down.

3. You need to study the context and framework of the verse carefully, to establish what the author meant by the words he used. In other words, find the beginning and the end of the context that your passage falls within.

4. You need to understand exegesis: find the historical setting, determine author intent, study key words, and note parallel passages. You need to slow down and carefully read the account, considering exactly what is being said

5. You need to find a reasonable harmonization of parallel passages.

6. You need to consider a variety of trusted Bible commentaries, dictionaries, lexical sources, encyclopedias, as well as books on Bible difficulties.

7. You should investigate as to whether the difficulty is a transmission error in the original text.

8. You must always keep in mind that the historical accuracy of the biblical text is unmatched; that thousands of extant manuscripts some of which date back to the second century B.C. support the transmitted text of Scripture.

9. We must keep in mind that the Bible is a diverse book when it comes to literary styles: narrative, poetic, prophetic, and apocalyptic; also containing parables, metaphors, similes, hyperbole, and other figures of speech. Too often, these alleged errors are the result of a reader taking a figure of speech as literal or reading a parable as though it is a narrative.

10. The Bible student needs to understand what level that the Bible intends to be exact in what is written. If Jim told a friend that 650 graduated with him from high school in 1984, it is not challenged, because it is all too clear that he is using rounded numbers and is not meaning to be precise.

CHAPTER 13 How Can We Know the Bible Is Authentic and True?

The Inspiration and Inerrancy of Scripture

The authenticity and truth of the Bible are rooted in the belief that it is the inspired and inerrant Word of God. 2 Timothy 3:16-17 states, "All Scripture is inspired by God and beneficial for teaching, for reproof, for correction, for training in righteousness; so that the man of God may be adequate, equipped for every good work." The term "inspired by God" (Greek: theopneustos) literally means "God-breathed," indicating that the Scriptures originate from God Himself. Consequently, they are trustworthy and reliable.

Moreover, 2 Peter 1:21 reinforces the divine origin of Scripture: "For no prophecy was ever made by an act of human will, but men moved by the Holy Spirit spoke from God." This passage highlights that the human authors of the Bible wrote under the guidance of the Holy Spirit, ensuring that their writings were free from error. The inerrancy of the Bible, therefore, is not a claim about every copy or translation but about the original autographs.

Historical Reliability of the Bible

The historical reliability of the Bible is a critical aspect of its authenticity. The Bible contains numerous historical accounts that have been corroborated by archaeological discoveries and external historical records.

Archaeological Evidence

Archaeology has provided substantial evidence supporting the historical reliability of the Bible. For instance, the discovery of the Dead Sea Scrolls in 1947 significantly bolstered the textual integrity of the Old Testament, demonstrating that the biblical texts have been faithfully preserved over millennia.

The Hittites, mentioned numerous times in the Old Testament (Genesis 23:10; 2 Samuel 11:3), were once thought to be a mythical people due to the lack of historical evidence. However, archaeological excavations in the early 20th century uncovered extensive records of the Hittite civilization, confirming their existence and corroborating the biblical narrative.

The Pool of Bethesda, where Jesus healed a man who had been infirm for 38 years (John 5:1-15), was long considered a symbolic or mythical location. However, excavations in Jerusalem have revealed the pool with its five porticoes, matching the description in John's Gospel and validating the historical accuracy of the account.

External Historical Sources

External historical sources from non-Christian writers also provide evidence for the historical reliability of the Bible. Tacitus, a Roman historian, wrote about the persecution of Christians under Nero and mentioned Christus (Christ) who "suffered the extreme penalty during the reign of Tiberius at the hands of one of our procurators, Pontius Pilate." This aligns with the New Testament accounts of Jesus' crucifixion and the subsequent growth of the Christian movement.

Josephus, a first-century Jewish historian, also references Jesus and His followers. In his work "Antiquities of the Jews," Josephus writes, "At this time there was a wise man who was called Jesus. And his conduct was good, and he was known to be virtuous. And many people from among the Jews and the other nations became his disciples. Pilate condemned him to be crucified and to die. But those who had become his disciples did not abandon his discipleship. They reported that he had appeared to them three days after his crucifixion and that he was alive."

Fulfillment of Prophecy

The fulfillment of prophecy is a unique characteristic of the Bible that provides strong evidence for its divine inspiration and authenticity. The Bible contains numerous prophecies that have been fulfilled with remarkable accuracy, demonstrating that they are not the result of human guesswork but of divine revelation.

IS THE BIBLE REALLY THE WORD OF GOD?

Messianic Prophecies

One of the most compelling areas of fulfilled prophecy is the Messianic prophecies—predictions about the coming of the Messiah, Jesus Christ. These prophecies, found throughout the Old Testament, were fulfilled in the life, death, and resurrection of Jesus, providing strong evidence for the reliability of Scripture.

Birthplace of the Messiah

The prophet Micah, writing around 700 B.C.E., foretold that the Messiah would be born in Bethlehem. Micah 5:2 states, "But as for you, Bethlehem Ephrathah, too little to be among the clans of Judah, from you One will go forth for Me to be ruler in Israel. His goings forth are from long ago, from the days of eternity." This prophecy was fulfilled in the birth of Jesus, as recorded in Matthew 2:1, "Now after Jesus was born in Bethlehem of Judea in the days of Herod the king, magi from the east arrived in Jerusalem."

The Virgin Birth

Isaiah 7:14 prophesied the virgin birth of the Messiah, "Therefore Jehovah Himself will give you a sign: Behold, a virgin will be with child and bear a son, and she will call His name Immanuel." This prophecy was fulfilled in the birth of Jesus, as described in Matthew 1:22-23, "Now all this took place to fulfill what was spoken by Jehovah through the prophet: 'Behold, the virgin shall be with child and shall bear a son, and they shall call His name Immanuel,' which translated means, 'God with us.'"

Betrayal for Thirty Pieces of Silver

Zechariah 11:12-13 predicted the betrayal of the Messiah for thirty pieces of silver, "I said to them, 'If it is good in your sight, give me my wages; but if not, never mind!' So they weighed out thirty shekels of silver as my wages. Then Jehovah said to me, 'Throw it to the potter, that magnificent price at which I was valued by them.' So I took the thirty shekels of silver and threw them to the potter in the house of Jehovah." This prophecy was fulfilled in the betrayal of Jesus by Judas Iscariot, as recorded in Matthew 26:14-15, "Then one of the twelve, named Judas Iscariot, went to the chief priests and said, 'What are you willing to give me to betray Him to you?' And they weighed out thirty pieces of silver to him."

Crucifixion Details

Psalm 22, written by David around 1000 B.C.E., contains several detailed prophecies about the crucifixion of the Messiah. Psalm 22:16-18 states, "For dogs have surrounded me; a band of evildoers has encompassed me; they pierced my hands and my feet. I can count all my bones. They look, they stare at me; they divide my garments among them, and for my clothing they cast lots." These details were fulfilled in the crucifixion of Jesus, as described in John 19:23-24, "Then the soldiers, when they had crucified Jesus, took His outer garments and made four parts, a part to every soldier and also the tunic; now the tunic was seamless, woven in one piece. So they said to one another, 'Let us not tear it, but cast lots for it, to decide whose it shall be.' This was to fulfill the Scripture: 'They divided My outer garments among them, and for My clothing they cast lots.'"

Resurrection Prophecy

The resurrection of Jesus was also prophesied in the Old Testament. Psalm 16:10 states, "For You will not abandon my soul to Sheol; nor will You allow Your Holy One to undergo decay." This prophecy was fulfilled in the resurrection of Jesus, as Peter explained in Acts 2:31-32, "he looked ahead and spoke of the resurrection of the Christ, that He was neither abandoned to Hades, nor did His flesh suffer decay. This Jesus God raised up again, to which we are all witnesses."

Consistency and Coherence of the Biblical Narrative

Despite being written over a span of 1,500 years by more than 40 authors from diverse backgrounds, the Bible exhibits remarkable consistency and coherence. This unity is evident in the overarching narrative of creation, fall, redemption, and restoration that runs throughout the Scriptures. The consistency of themes, prophecies, and teachings across different books and authors points to the divine inspiration of the Bible.

The Prophecy of the Suffering Servant

IS THE BIBLE REALLY THE WORD OF GOD?

The prophecy of the suffering servant in Isaiah 53, written around 700 B.C.E., finds its fulfillment in the New Testament account of Jesus' crucifixion. Isaiah 53:5 states, "But he was pierced through for our transgressions, he was crushed for our iniquities; the chastening for our well-being fell upon him, and by his scourging we are healed." The precise fulfillment of this prophecy in the life and death of Jesus underscores the coherence and reliability of the biblical narrative.

The Unity of Biblical Themes

The Bible's consistent themes of God's sovereignty, human sin, and the need for redemption demonstrate its divine authorship. The narrative of creation in Genesis, the promise of a Messiah in the prophets, the incarnation of Jesus in the Gospels, and the promise of eternal life in Revelation all contribute to a cohesive and unified message. This thematic unity across diverse authors and historical contexts indicates that the Bible is the product of a singular divine mind.

Textual Integrity and Manuscript Evidence

The textual integrity of the Bible is another critical aspect of its authenticity. Despite the passage of time and the process of transmission, the Bible has been remarkably well-preserved.

Old Testament Manuscripts

The discovery of the Dead Sea Scrolls, dating from the third century B.C.E. to the first century C.E., provided significant evidence for the reliability of the Old Testament text. The scrolls include portions of almost every book of the Old Testament and demonstrate that the text has been transmitted with great fidelity over the centuries.

New Testament Manuscripts

The New Testament is supported by a wealth of manuscript evidence, with over 5,800 Greek manuscripts, 10,000 Latin manuscripts, and numerous others in various languages. The sheer volume and early dating of these manuscripts allow scholars to reconstruct the original text with a high degree of accuracy. For example, the Rylands Library Papyrus P52, dated to around 125 C.E., contains a fragment of the Gospel of John and provides evidence for the early circulation of the New Testament writings.

Internal Consistency and Eyewitness Testimony

The internal consistency of the Bible and the eyewitness testimony of its authors provide further evidence of its authenticity.

Consistency of the Gospel Accounts

The Gospels of Matthew, Mark, Luke, and John present a consistent portrait of Jesus, despite their different perspectives and audiences. While there are variations in the details, these differences do not constitute contradictions but rather provide a fuller picture of Jesus' life and ministry. The core message of Jesus' death, resurrection, and divinity remains consistent across all four accounts.

Eyewitness Testimony

The New Testament writers often emphasize their roles as eyewitnesses to the events they describe. John 1:14 states, "And the Word became flesh, and dwelt among us, and we saw His glory, glory as of the only begotten from the Father, full of grace and truth." Similarly, 1 John 1:1-3 emphasizes the eyewitness nature of John's testimony: "What was from the beginning, what we have heard, what we have seen with our eyes, what we have looked at and touched with our hands, concerning the Word of Life... we proclaim to you also."

Peter also stresses the importance of eyewitness testimony in 2 Peter 1:16, "For we did not follow cleverly devised tales when we made known to you the power and coming of our Lord Jesus Christ, but we were eyewitnesses of His majesty." The emphasis on firsthand accounts strengthens the credibility of the biblical narrative.

Addressing Common Objections

Critics often raise objections to the authenticity and truth of the Bible, including claims of contradictions, scientific inaccuracies, and ethical concerns. These objections can be addressed through careful examination of the text and a proper understanding of its context.

Alleged Contradictions

IS THE BIBLE REALLY THE WORD OF GOD?

Many alleged contradictions in the Bible can be resolved through a careful examination of the context, language, and cultural background. For example, the different genealogies of Jesus presented in Matthew 1 and Luke 3 have been cited as a contradiction. However, a common explanation is that Matthew records Joseph's genealogy, emphasizing Jesus' legal right to David's throne, while Luke records Mary's genealogy, emphasizing Jesus' biological descent from David.

Scientific Statements in the Bible

The Bible, though not a scientific textbook, contains insights and statements that align with scientific discoveries made thousands of years later. These insights demonstrate the advanced understanding of natural phenomena in the Scriptures, providing further evidence of their divine inspiration.

For example, Isaiah 40:22 states, "It is He who sits above the circle of the earth, and its inhabitants are like grasshoppers, who stretches out the heavens like a curtain and spreads them out like a tent to dwell in." This reference to the "circle of the earth" aligns with the understanding that the earth is spherical, a fact not commonly accepted until much later in history.

Job 26:7 provides further insight into the earth's position in space: "He stretches out the north over empty space and hangs the earth on nothing." This description accurately portrays the earth as suspended in space, a concept that aligns with modern astronomical understanding.

Ethical Concerns

Ethical concerns, such as the Bible's depiction of violence or its treatment of women and slavery, must be understood in their historical and cultural context. The Bible records the realities of ancient societies and God's redemptive work within those contexts. While certain practices described in the Bible reflect the cultural norms of the time, the overarching biblical narrative reveals God's progressive revelation of justice, mercy, and love.

Romans 2:14-15 explains that God's moral law is written on the hearts of all people: "For when Gentiles who do not have the Law do instinctively the things of the Law, these, not having the Law, are a law to themselves, in that they show the work of the Law written in their hearts, their conscience bearing witness and their thoughts alternately accusing or else defending them." This passage highlights the universal and objective nature of biblical morality, which resonates with the human conscience.

The Role of Faith and Reason

While historical, contextual, and textual analyses provide substantial evidence for the authenticity and truth of the Bible, faith also plays a crucial role in accepting these truths. Hebrews 11:1 defines faith as "the assurance of things hoped for, the conviction of things not seen." Faith in the Bible's reliability is not contrary to reason but is supported by reasonable evidence and the internal witness of the Holy Spirit.

Christian apologetics bridges the gap between faith and reason, demonstrating that belief in the Bible is intellectually viable and spiritually enriching. As 1 Peter 3:15 exhorts, "But sanctify Christ as Lord in your hearts, always being ready to make a defense to everyone who asks you to give an account for the hope that is in you, yet with gentleness and reverence." This call to defend the faith includes providing well-reasoned answers to challenges regarding the authenticity and truth of the Bible.

CHAPTER 14 How is the Bible Is Practical for Our Day?

The Timeless Wisdom of the Bible

The Bible, though written thousands of years ago, contains timeless wisdom that remains relevant and practical for our daily lives. Its teachings address fundamental human concerns, offering guidance on morality, relationships, work, and spirituality. As 2 Timothy 3:16-17 states, "All Scripture is inspired by God and beneficial for teaching, for reproof, for correction, for training in righteousness; so that the man of God may be adequate, equipped for every good work." This passage highlights the practical benefits of Scripture for living a righteous and fulfilling life.

Moral and Ethical Guidance

One of the most practical aspects of the Bible is its moral and ethical guidance. The Ten Commandments (Exodus 20:1-17) and the teachings of Jesus, such as the Sermon on the Mount (Matthew 5-7), provide clear principles for righteous living. These teachings address issues like honesty, integrity, love, forgiveness, and justice, which are crucial for building a healthy and just society.

The Greatest Commandments

Jesus summarized the moral law in two commandments: "You shall love Jehovah your God with all your heart, and with all your soul, and with all your mind. This is the great and foremost commandment. The second is like it, You shall love your neighbor as yourself" (Matthew 22:37-39). These commandments encapsulate the essence of ethical behavior, emphasizing the importance of love for God and others.

Practical Applications

- **Honesty and Integrity**: Proverbs 12:22 states, "Lying lips are an abomination to Jehovah, but those who deal faithfully are

His delight." This principle encourages honesty in all our dealings, fostering trust and reliability in personal and professional relationships.

- **Forgiveness and Reconciliation**: Ephesians 4:32 advises, "Be kind to one another, tender-hearted, forgiving each other, just as God in Christ also has forgiven you." Practicing forgiveness leads to healthier relationships and emotional well-being.

- **Justice and Fairness**: Micah 6:8 declares, "He has told you, O man, what is good; and what does Jehovah require of you but to do justice, to love kindness, and to walk humbly with your God?" This verse emphasizes the importance of justice and kindness, guiding us to treat others fairly and compassionately.

Guidance for Relationships

The Bible provides profound insights into building and maintaining healthy relationships. Its teachings on love, respect, and commitment are essential for fostering strong and lasting bonds in families, friendships, and communities.

Marriage and Family

Ephesians 5:22-33 offers practical advice for husbands and wives, emphasizing mutual love and respect. "Husbands, love your wives, just as Christ also loved the church and gave Himself up for her" (Ephesians 5:25). This passage encourages sacrificial love and selflessness in marriage, principles that strengthen the marital bond.

Parenting

Proverbs 22:6 advises, "Train up a child in the way he should go, even when he is old he will not depart from it." This verse underscores the importance of nurturing and guiding children with wisdom and love, laying a strong foundation for their future.

Friendship

Proverbs 17:17 states, "A friend loves at all times, and a brother is born for adversity." This highlights the value of loyalty and support in friendships, essential qualities for building deep and meaningful connections.

Practical Wisdom for Work and Finances

The Bible also provides practical wisdom for managing work and finances. Its teachings encourage diligence, integrity, and stewardship, principles that lead to success and fulfillment in our professional and financial endeavors.

Diligence and Hard Work

Proverbs 13:4 states, "The soul of the sluggard craves and gets nothing, but the soul of the diligent is made fat." This verse highlights the value of hard work and perseverance, qualities that are essential for achieving our goals and fulfilling our responsibilities.

Integrity in Business

Proverbs 11:1 declares, "A false balance is an abomination to Jehovah, but a just weight is His delight." This principle encourages honesty and fairness in business dealings, fostering trust and ethical practices.

Stewardship and Generosity

1 Timothy 6:17-19 advises, "Instruct those who are rich in this present world not to be conceited or to fix their hope on the uncertainty of riches, but on God, who richly supplies us with all things to enjoy. Instruct them to do good, to be rich in good works, to be generous and ready to share." This passage underscores the importance of wise stewardship and generosity, guiding us to use our resources for the benefit of others and the glory of God.

Emotional and Mental Well-being

The Bible offers profound insights into emotional and mental well-being, providing comfort, hope, and strength in times of distress. Its teachings encourage a positive outlook on life, grounded in faith and trust in God.

Overcoming Anxiety

Philippians 4:6-7 advises, "Be anxious for nothing, but in everything by prayer and supplication with thanksgiving let your requests be made known to God. And the peace of God, which surpasses all comprehension, will guard your hearts and your minds in Christ Jesus." This passage encourages us to turn to God in prayer, finding peace and relief from anxiety through His presence.

Finding Hope

Jeremiah 29:11 provides a message of hope, "For I know the plans that I have for you, declares Jehovah, plans for welfare and not for calamity to give you a future and a hope." This assurance of God's good plans for our future offers hope and encouragement, especially in difficult times.

Strength in Weakness

Isaiah 40:31 declares, "Yet those who wait for Jehovah will gain new strength; they will mount up with wings like eagles, they will run and not get tired, they will walk and not become weary." This verse reminds us that our strength comes from God, who renews and sustains us through life's challenges.

Spiritual Growth and Fulfillment

The Bible is a profound guide for spiritual growth and fulfillment. Its teachings lead us to a deeper relationship with God, providing the foundation for a meaningful and purposeful life.

Knowing God

Jeremiah 9:23-24 emphasizes the importance of knowing God, "Thus says Jehovah, 'Let not a wise man boast of his wisdom, and let not the mighty man boast of his might, let not a rich man boast of his riches; but let him who boasts boast of this, that he understands and knows Me, that I am Jehovah who exercises lovingkindness, justice and righteousness on earth; for I delight in these things,' declares Jehovah." Knowing God and understanding His character is the foundation of true wisdom and fulfillment.

Spiritual Discipline

IS THE BIBLE REALLY THE WORD OF GOD?

1 Timothy 4:7-8 advises, "But have nothing to do with worldly fables fit only for old women. On the other hand, discipline yourself for the purpose of godliness; for bodily discipline is only of little profit, but godliness is profitable for all things, since it holds promise for the present life and also for the life to come." Spiritual disciplines such as prayer, meditation on Scripture, and worship cultivate godliness and deepen our relationship with God.

Living with Purpose

Ephesians 2:10 states, "For we are His workmanship, created in Christ Jesus for good works, which God prepared beforehand so that we would walk in them." This verse emphasizes that we are created with a purpose, called to live out God's plans for our lives through good works and service to others.

Practical Guidance for Society

The Bible's teachings extend beyond individual lives, offering practical guidance for building just and compassionate societies. Its principles of justice, mercy, and love are foundational for social harmony and the common good.

Justice and Righteousness

Amos 5:24 calls for justice, "But let justice roll down like waters and righteousness like an ever-flowing stream." This principle guides us to pursue justice and righteousness in our communities, advocating for fairness and equity.

Compassion and Mercy

Micah 6:8 again emphasizes the importance of compassion, "He has told you, O man, what is good; and what does Jehovah require of you but to do justice, to love kindness, and to walk humbly with your God?" Practicing compassion and mercy towards others fosters social cohesion and mutual support.

Community and Fellowship

Acts 2:42-47 describes the early Christian community, "They were continually devoting themselves to the apostles' teaching and to fellowship, to the breaking of bread and to prayer... And all those who had believed were together and had all things in common; and they began selling their property and possessions and were sharing them with all, as anyone might have need." This model of community and fellowship encourages us to support one another, share resources, and build strong, caring communities.

The Role of Faith and Reason

While the Bible provides practical guidance for many aspects of life, faith plays a crucial role in accepting and applying its teachings. Hebrews 11:1 defines faith as "the assurance of things hoped for, the conviction of things not seen." Faith in the Bible's teachings is supported by reasonable evidence and the internal witness of the Holy Spirit.

Christian apologetics bridges the gap between faith and reason, demonstrating that belief in the Bible is intellectually viable and spiritually enriching. As 1 Peter 3:15 exhorts, "But sanctify Christ as Lord in your hearts, always being ready to make a defense to everyone who asks you to give an account for the hope that is in you, yet with gentleness and reverence." This call to defend the faith includes providing well-reasoned answers to challenges regarding the practicality of the Bible's teachings.

The Testimony of Jesus and the Apostles

The testimony of Jesus and the apostles provides additional assurance of the Bible's practicality and relevance. Jesus affirmed the authority and reliability of the Scriptures, stating in Matthew 5:18, "For truly I say to you, until heaven and earth pass away, not the smallest letter or stroke shall pass from the Law until all is accomplished." Jesus' endorsement of the Scriptures as trustworthy and enduring underscores their divine origin and practicality.

The apostles also affirmed the practicality of Scripture. Peter, in 2 Peter 1:3, emphasizes that God's divine power has granted us "everything pertaining to life and godliness, through the true knowledge of Him who called us by His own glory and excellence." Paul, in 2 Timothy 3:16, asserts the usefulness and divine origin of all Scripture, emphasizing its role in equipping believers for every good work.

CHAPTER 15 Infallibility and Absolute Inerrancy of Scripture, Really?

The Doctrine of Infallibility and Inerrancy

The doctrine of the infallibility and inerrancy of Scripture asserts that the Bible, in its original manuscripts, is without error in all that it affirms, whether pertaining to doctrine, history, science, geography, or any other discipline. 2 Timothy 3:16 states, "All Scripture is inspired by God and beneficial for teaching, for reproof, for correction, for training in righteousness," indicating that the Bible is wholly reliable and authoritative.

However, many modern liberal scholars challenge this doctrine, asserting that the Bible contains errors and inconsistencies. This article will examine some of these claims and provide a conservative evangelical response, affirming the trustworthiness and inerrancy of Scripture.

Claims of Liberal Scholars

Liberal scholars often argue that the Bible is fallible and errant based on perceived contradictions, historical inaccuracies, and scientific discrepancies. These scholars include Bart D. Ehrman, John Dominic Crossan, and Richard Elliott Friedman, among others.

Bart D. Ehrman

Bart D. Ehrman, a well-known New Testament scholar, argues that the Bible is full of contradictions and textual alterations. In his book "Misquoting Jesus," Ehrman asserts that scribes who copied the biblical manuscripts made numerous changes, leading to significant textual variations. He claims these changes undermine the reliability of the New Testament.

John Dominic Crossan

John Dominic Crossan, a prominent member of the Jesus Seminar, argues that the Gospel accounts are not historically reliable. In his book "The Birth of Christianity," Crossan contends that the resurrection of Jesus is a metaphorical rather than a historical event. He suggests that the Gospel writers created narratives to convey theological truths rather than historical facts.

Richard Elliott Friedman

Richard Elliott Friedman, a biblical scholar known for his work on the Documentary Hypothesis, argues that the Pentateuch (the first five books of the Old Testament) is a composite work written by multiple authors over several centuries. In his book "Who Wrote the Bible?" Friedman claims that the inconsistencies and contradictions within the Pentateuch indicate it is not a unified, divinely inspired text.

Refuting the Claims of Liberal Scholars

While these scholars present their arguments, a closer examination reveals that their claims often rest on assumptions and interpretative biases rather than definitive evidence. Here, we address and refute their primary assertions.

Textual Variations and Inerrancy

Bart Ehrman's argument about textual variations does not necessarily undermine the doctrine of inerrancy. While it is true that scribes made changes to the manuscripts, the vast majority of these variations are minor and do not affect the essential doctrines of the Christian faith. Textual criticism, the scholarly discipline that examines these variations, has demonstrated that we can reconstruct the original text of the New Testament with a high degree of accuracy.

For example, Daniel B. Wallace, a conservative textual critic, points out that over 99% of the textual variations in the New Testament are inconsequential, such as differences in spelling or word order. The essential message and core doctrines of the New Testament remain intact. Moreover, the sheer number of New Testament manuscripts (over 5,800 Greek manuscripts) provides a robust basis for reconstructing the original text.

Historical Reliability of the Gospels

IS THE BIBLE REALLY THE WORD OF GOD?

John Dominic Crossan's claim that the resurrection of Jesus is metaphorical rather than historical lacks substantial evidence. The New Testament provides multiple independent accounts of the resurrection, including the Gospels, Acts, and Paul's letters. These accounts are corroborated by early Christian creeds, such as the one found in 1 Corinthians 15:3-8, which dates to within a few years of the crucifixion.

Moreover, the historical evidence for the resurrection is compelling. Scholars such as N.T. Wright have argued that the resurrection is the best explanation for the empty tomb, the transformation of the disciples, and the rapid growth of the early church. The resurrection narratives contain details that would be unlikely to be fabricated, such as the testimony of women, who were considered unreliable witnesses in the first century.

Unity and Authorship of the Pentateuch

Richard Elliott Friedman's Documentary Hypothesis suggests that the Pentateuch is a patchwork of sources (J, E, P, D) compiled over centuries. However, this hypothesis is not universally accepted and has been challenged by conservative scholars who argue for the Mosaic authorship and unity of the Pentateuch.

One key argument against the Documentary Hypothesis is the consistent theological themes and literary structures found throughout the Pentateuch. For example, the covenantal framework, which begins with God's covenant with Abraham (Genesis 12, 15, 17) and continues through the Mosaic covenant (Exodus 19-24), suggests a unified narrative rather than a compilation of disparate sources.

Additionally, Jesus and the New Testament writers affirm the Mosaic authorship of the Pentateuch. In John 5:46-47, Jesus says, "For if you believed Moses, you would believe Me, for he wrote about Me. But if you do not believe his writings, how will you believe My words?" This affirmation by Jesus supports the traditional view of Mosaic authorship and the unity of the Pentateuch.

Addressing Specific Allegations of Error

Liberal scholars often cite specific examples they believe to be errors or contradictions in the Bible. Here, we address a few of these allegations.

Contradictions in the Resurrection Accounts

Critics argue that the resurrection accounts in the Gospels contain discrepancies, such as the number of women at the tomb or the sequence of events. However, these differences can be harmonized through careful examination. For instance, varying details about the women at the tomb reflect different perspectives and emphases of the Gospel writers rather than outright contradictions.

The core facts remain consistent across all four Gospels: Jesus was crucified, buried, the tomb was found empty, and He appeared to His followers after His resurrection. These consistent elements provide a strong basis for the historical reliability of the resurrection accounts.

Scientific Discrepancies

Some scholars argue that the Bible contains scientific errors, such as the creation account in Genesis. However, the Bible is not a scientific textbook but a theological document that conveys spiritual truths. The creation account, when understood in its literary and cultural context, provides profound theological insights about God's sovereignty and the goodness of His creation.

Moreover, many alleged scientific discrepancies are based on misunderstandings or misinterpretations of the text. For example, the Bible's description of the earth "hanging on nothing" (Job 26:7) aligns remarkably well with modern scientific understanding of the earth in space.

Ethical Issues

Critics also raise ethical concerns about the Bible, such as its treatment of women or the endorsement of slavery. However, these criticisms often fail to consider the historical and cultural context of the biblical texts. The Bible's ethical teachings must be understood in light of its redemptive trajectory, which progressively reveals God's will for justice, mercy, and love.

IS THE BIBLE REALLY THE WORD OF GOD?

For instance, while the Bible contains laws regulating slavery, it also sows the seeds for its eventual abolition. The New Testament, particularly Paul's letter to Philemon, emphasizes the inherent dignity and equality of all people in Christ (Galatians 3:28). Similarly, the Bible's treatment of women, while reflecting its historical context, includes radical affirmations of women's worth and roles, culminating in the New Testament's declaration that "there is neither male nor female; for you are all one in Christ Jesus" (Galatians 3:28).

The Testimony of Jesus and the Apostles

The testimony of Jesus and the apostles provides a strong foundation for the doctrine of inerrancy. Jesus affirmed the authority and reliability of the Scriptures, stating in Matthew 5:18, "For truly I say to you, until heaven and earth pass away, not the smallest letter or stroke shall pass from the Law until all is accomplished." Jesus' endorsement of the Scriptures as trustworthy and enduring underscores their divine origin and reliability.

The apostles also affirmed the inerrancy of Scripture. Peter, in 2 Peter 1:21, emphasizes the prophetic nature of Scripture and its divine inspiration: "For no prophecy was ever made by an act of human will, but men moved by the Holy Spirit spoke from God." Paul, in 2 Timothy 3:16, asserts the usefulness and divine origin of all Scripture, emphasizing its role in equipping believers for every good work.

Conclusion on the Infallibility and Inerrancy of Scripture

The claims of liberal scholars that the Bible is fallible and errant are not supported by a careful examination of the evidence. While there are challenges and complexities in the biblical text, these do not undermine the doctrine of inerrancy. The Bible, when understood in its historical, cultural, and literary context, remains a reliable and authoritative revelation of God's truth.

Edward D. Andrews

CHAPTER 16 Is the Word of God Really Alive?

The Living and Active Nature of Scripture

The assertion that the Word of God is alive and active is rooted in Hebrews 4:12, which states, "For the word of God is living and active and sharper than any two-edged sword, and piercing as far as the division of soul and spirit, of both joints and marrow, and able to judge the thoughts and intentions of the heart." This verse underscores the dynamic and transformative power of Scripture, asserting that it is not merely a historical document but a living force that interacts with believers in profound ways.

Transformative Power of the Word

The Bible's transformative power is evident in its ability to change lives. Through the reading and application of Scripture, individuals experience spiritual growth, moral improvement, and a deeper relationship with God. The transformative nature of the Word of God can be seen in numerous testimonies of changed lives throughout history.

Conversion of Paul

The conversion of Saul of Tarsus, later known as Paul, is one of the most dramatic examples of the Bible's transformative power. Paul was a zealous persecutor of Christians, but after encountering the risen Christ on the road to Damascus, his life was radically changed. He became one of the most influential apostles, spreading the gospel throughout the Roman Empire. In Galatians 1:23-24, Paul recounts, "But only, they kept hearing, 'He who once persecuted us is now preaching the faith which he once tried to destroy.' And they were glorifying God because of me." Paul's transformation illustrates the power of God's Word to change even the hardest of hearts.

The Ethiopian Eunuch

IS THE BIBLE REALLY THE WORD OF GOD?

Another powerful example is the story of the Ethiopian eunuch in Acts 8:26-39. As the eunuch was reading the book of Isaiah, Philip, guided by the Holy Spirit, explained the Scriptures to him. The eunuch's heart was opened, and he believed in Jesus Christ, leading to his immediate baptism. This story demonstrates how the Word of God, when properly understood, leads to faith and transformation.

The Word as Spiritual Nourishment

The Bible frequently describes itself as spiritual food that nourishes and sustains believers. Just as physical food is essential for physical health, the Word of God is essential for spiritual health.

Jesus, the Bread of Life

Jesus declared in John 6:35, "I am the bread of life; he who comes to Me will not hunger, and he who believes in Me will never thirst." This statement highlights the sustenance that comes from a relationship with Christ, mediated through His Word. The Scriptures provide the spiritual nourishment needed for believers to grow in their faith and remain steadfast in their walk with God.

Milk and Solid Food

The apostle Peter encourages believers to crave the pure milk of the Word. In 1 Peter 2:2-3, he writes, "Like newborn babies, long for the pure milk of the word, so that by it you may grow in respect to salvation, if you have tasted the kindness of the Lord." This analogy emphasizes the importance of Scripture for spiritual growth and maturity. Similarly, the writer of Hebrews contrasts milk with solid food, indicating that mature believers should move beyond basic teachings to deeper understanding and application of God's Word (Hebrews 5:12-14).

Guidance and Wisdom

The Bible provides guidance and wisdom for all aspects of life. Its teachings are timeless and relevant, offering direction for personal decisions, relationships, and moral dilemmas.

A Lamp to Our Feet

Psalm 119:105 states, "Your word is a lamp to my feet and a light to my path." This metaphor illustrates how the Scriptures guide believers through life's challenges and uncertainties. By illuminating the path before us, the Bible helps us make wise and godly decisions.

Wisdom for Life

Proverbs is a book filled with practical wisdom for daily living. Proverbs 3:5-6 advises, "Trust in Jehovah with all your heart and do not lean on your own understanding. In all your ways acknowledge Him, and He will make your paths straight." This counsel emphasizes the importance of relying on God's wisdom rather than our own. The principles found in Proverbs cover a wide range of topics, including relationships, work, finances, and personal conduct, providing timeless advice that remains applicable today.

Conviction and Correction

The Word of God also serves as a tool for conviction and correction. It reveals our sins and shortcomings, leading us to repentance and growth in righteousness.

Sharper than a Two-Edged Sword

Hebrews 4:12 describes the Word of God as "sharper than any two-edged sword." This imagery conveys the penetrating power of Scripture to expose the innermost thoughts and intentions of the heart. As we read and meditate on God's Word, it convicts us of sin and challenges us to live in accordance with His will.

Reproof and Correction

2 Timothy 3:16-17 highlights the role of Scripture in reproof and correction: "All Scripture is inspired by God and beneficial for teaching, for reproof, for correction, for training in righteousness; so that the man of God may be adequate, equipped for every good work." The Bible not only points out where we have gone wrong but also provides the guidance and instruction needed to correct our behavior and grow in godliness.

The Role of the Holy Spirit

IS THE BIBLE REALLY THE WORD OF GOD?

The Holy Spirit plays a crucial role in making the Word of God alive and active in the lives of believers. The Spirit illuminates the Scriptures, helping us to understand and apply them to our lives.

Illumination

Understanding how we receive illumination and guidance from God is rooted in the inspired, inerrant Word of God. According to 1 Corinthians 2:12-14, the process involves more than merely acquiring a mental grasp of biblical truths; it requires embracing these truths as divinely revealed. The expressions "does not accept," "folly," and "not able to understand" highlight how unbelievers critique and reject divine revelation. This passage does not imply that unbelievers are incapable of understanding the Bible's content; rather, they view it as foolishness. Christians, however, are guided by having the mind of Christ (1 Corinthians 2:16), achieved through being biblically minded. This necessitates a careful analysis of the Bible's genres, historical context, and language, employing the conservative, objective historical-grammatical method of interpretation while avoiding the speculative fallacies of modern biblical criticism.

Empowerment

The Holy Spirit also empowers believers to live out the teachings of Scripture. In Acts 1:8, Jesus told His disciples, "But you will receive power when the Holy Spirit has come upon you; and you shall be My witnesses both in Jerusalem, and in all Judea and Samaria, and even to the remotest part of the earth." The Spirit equips us with the strength and courage needed to obey God's Word and fulfill His purposes.

The Eternal Nature of the Word

The Bible emphasizes the eternal nature of God's Word, affirming that it will never pass away. This eternal quality underscores the reliability and enduring relevance of Scripture.

The Word Endures Forever

Isaiah 40:8 declares, "The grass withers, the flower fades, but the word of our God stands forever." This verse highlights the permanence of God's Word in contrast to the transience of the natural world. Jesus echoed this truth in Matthew 24:35, saying, "Heaven and earth will pass away, but My words will not pass away."

Living and Enduring Word

1 Peter 1:23-25 emphasizes the living and enduring nature of the Word: "For you have been born again not of seed which is perishable but imperishable, that is, through the living and enduring word of God. For, 'All flesh is like grass, and all its glory like the flower of grass. The grass withers, and the flower falls off, but the word of the Lord endures forever.' And this is the word which was preached to you." The enduring nature of Scripture assures us that its truths remain relevant and authoritative across all generations.

The Impact on Society

The transformative power of God's Word extends beyond individuals to impact entire societies. Throughout history, the principles and teachings of the Bible have influenced laws, ethics, and social norms, leading to positive change and progress.

Abolition of Slavery

The Bible's teachings on the inherent worth and dignity of every human being have played a significant role in movements for social justice, such as the abolition of slavery. Christian abolitionists, inspired by the Scriptures, worked tirelessly to end the practice of slavery. Key verses, such as Galatians 3:28, which declares, "There is neither Jew nor Greek, there is neither slave nor free man, there is neither male nor female; for you are all one in Christ Jesus," motivated and guided their efforts.

Human Rights and Dignity

The biblical concept of humans being made in the image of God (Genesis 1:27) has profoundly influenced the development of human rights and the recognition of human dignity. This principle undergirds many modern legal and ethical systems, promoting the inherent value and equality of all people.

Charitable Work and Social Services

The teachings of Jesus and the apostles on love, compassion, and service have inspired countless charitable organizations and social services. Hospitals, orphanages, and humanitarian agencies founded by Christians continue to provide care and support to those in need. James 1:27 emphasizes the importance of caring for the vulnerable:

IS THE BIBLE REALLY THE WORD OF GOD?

"Pure and undefiled religion in the sight of our God and Father is this: to visit orphans and widows in their distress, and to keep oneself unstained by the world."

The Word in Personal Spiritual Practice

The Bible is not only a source of doctrinal truth and historical record but also a vital tool for personal spiritual practice. It provides guidance for prayer, meditation, and worship, fostering a deeper relationship with God.

Prayer

Scripture guides us in how to pray and what to pray for. The Lord's Prayer, taught by Jesus in Matthew 6:9-13, serves as a model for our prayers, emphasizing praise, petition, and submission to God's will. Additionally, the Psalms provide numerous examples of prayers that express a wide range of emotions and situations, from lament to thanksgiving.

Meditation

Meditating on God's Word allows us to internalize its truths and apply them to our lives. Psalm 1:2 describes the blessed person as one whose "delight is in the law of Jehovah, and in His law he meditates day and night." This practice of meditation fosters spiritual growth and deepens our understanding of God's will.

Worship

The Bible also informs and enriches our worship, providing songs, prayers, and liturgical elements that draw us closer to God. The book of Psalms, for instance, is a rich resource for both personal and corporate worship, expressing adoration, confession, and supplication.

The Testimony of Jesus and the Apostles

The testimony of Jesus and the apostles provides additional assurance of the Bible's living and active nature. Jesus affirmed the authority and reliability of the Scriptures, stating in Matthew 5:18, "For truly I say to you, until heaven and earth pass away, not the smallest letter or stroke shall pass from the Law until all is accomplished." Jesus' endorsement of the Scriptures as trustworthy and enduring underscores their divine origin and reliability.

The apostles also affirmed the living nature of God's Word. Peter, in 1 Peter 1:23-25, emphasizes the enduring quality of the Word: "For you have been born again not of seed which is perishable but imperishable, that is, through the living and enduring word of God." Paul, in 2 Timothy 3:16-17, asserts the usefulness and divine origin of all Scripture, emphasizing its role in equipping believers for every good work.

CHAPTER 17 How Does the Bible Relate to You?

The Divine Inspiration and Authority of the Bible

The Bible, as the inspired Word of God, holds a unique place of authority and relevance in the life of every believer. 2 Timothy 3:16-17 states, "All Scripture is inspired by God and beneficial for teaching, for reproof, for correction, for training in righteousness; so that the man of God may be adequate, equipped for every good work." This passage emphasizes that the Scriptures are not merely historical documents but are divinely inspired, providing essential guidance for every aspect of life.

Personal Relationship with God

One of the most profound ways the Bible relates to individuals is by fostering a personal relationship with God. Through the Scriptures, God reveals Himself, His character, and His will, inviting us into a deeper relationship with Him.

Revelation of God's Character

The Bible reveals God's attributes, such as His holiness, love, justice, and mercy. Exodus 34:6-7 declares, "Then Jehovah passed by in front of him and proclaimed, 'Jehovah, Jehovah God, compassionate and gracious, slow to anger, and abounding in lovingkindness and truth; who keeps lovingkindness for thousands, who forgives iniquity, transgression and sin; yet He will by no means leave the guilty unpunished, visiting the iniquity of fathers on the children and on the grandchildren to the third and fourth generations.'" This revelation of God's character helps us understand who He is and how we can relate to Him.

God's Plan for Salvation

The Bible outlines God's plan for salvation through Jesus Christ. John 3:16-17 proclaims, "For God so loved the world, that He gave

His only begotten Son, that whoever believes in Him shall not perish, but have eternal life. For God did not send the Son into the world to judge the world, but that the world might be saved through Him." This message of salvation is central to the Bible's relevance, offering hope and redemption to all who believe.

Guidance for Daily Living

The Bible provides practical guidance for daily living, addressing various aspects of life, including relationships, work, and moral conduct. Its teachings are timeless, offering wisdom and direction for contemporary challenges.

Wisdom for Relationships

The Bible offers profound insights into building and maintaining healthy relationships. Ephesians 4:2-3 advises, "With all humility and gentleness, with patience, showing tolerance for one another in love, being diligent to preserve the unity of the Spirit in the bond of peace." This counsel promotes harmonious relationships grounded in love and mutual respect.

Ethical Conduct

The Bible's ethical teachings guide believers in living upright and moral lives. Micah 6:8 encapsulates this, stating, "He has told you, O man, what is good; and what does Jehovah require of you but to do justice, to love kindness, and to walk humbly with your God?" This verse highlights the importance of justice, kindness, and humility in our daily conduct.

Work and Stewardship

The Bible also provides guidance on work and stewardship. Colossians 3:23-24 instructs, "Whatever you do, do your work heartily, as for the Lord rather than for men, knowing that from the Lord you will receive the reward of the inheritance. It is the Lord Christ whom you serve." This principle encourages diligence and integrity in our work, reminding us that we ultimately serve God.

Spiritual Growth and Maturity

IS THE BIBLE REALLY THE WORD OF GOD?

The Bible is a vital tool for spiritual growth and maturity, offering nourishment, correction, and encouragement to believers.

Spiritual Nourishment

Jesus described Himself as the bread of life, emphasizing the sustaining power of His Word. John 6:35 states, "Jesus said to them, 'I am the bread of life; he who comes to Me will not hunger, and he who believes in Me will never thirst.'" Just as physical food sustains our bodies, the Word of God sustains our spirits.

Correction and Reproof

The Bible serves as a mirror, revealing areas of our lives that need correction. James 1:23-25 illustrates this, "For if anyone is a hearer of the word and not a doer, he is like a man who looks at his natural face in a mirror; for once he has looked at himself and gone away, he has immediately forgotten what kind of person he was. But one who looks intently at the perfect law, the law of liberty, and abides by it, not having become a forgetful hearer but an effectual doer, this man will be blessed in what he does." Through Scripture, God convicts us of sin and guides us toward righteousness.

Encouragement and Hope

The Bible offers comfort and hope in times of distress. Romans 15:4 reminds us, "For whatever was written in earlier times was written for our instruction, so that through perseverance and the encouragement of the Scriptures we might have hope." The promises of God found in the Bible provide reassurance and strength to endure life's challenges.

The Role of the Holy Spirit

The Holy Spirit plays a crucial role in helping believers understand and apply the Bible to their lives. The Spirit illuminates the Scriptures, making them alive and active.

Illumination of Scripture

John 16:13 states, "But when He, the Spirit of truth, comes, He will guide you into all the truth; for He will not speak on His own initiative, but whatever He hears, He will speak; and He will disclose to you what is to come." The Holy Spirit helps believers understand the deep truths of God's Word and apply them to their lives.

Empowerment for Obedience

The Holy Spirit also empowers believers to live according to the teachings of Scripture. Galatians 5:22-23 describes the fruit of the Spirit, which includes love, joy, peace, patience, kindness, goodness, faithfulness, gentleness, and self-control. These qualities reflect a life transformed by the Spirit through the application of God's Word.

The Bible and Community

The Bible not only addresses individual believers but also provides guidance for the corporate life of the church. It shapes the community of faith, fostering unity, love, and mutual edification.

Unity in the Body of Christ

Ephesians 4:3-6 urges believers to maintain unity, "being diligent to preserve the unity of the Spirit in the bond of peace. There is one body and one Spirit, just as also you were called in one hope of your calling; one Lord, one faith, one baptism, one God and Father of all who is over all and through all and in all." The Bible's teachings promote unity within the church, encouraging believers to work together harmoniously.

Mutual Edification

The Bible also emphasizes the importance of building one another up in the faith. Hebrews 10:24-25 states, "and let us consider how to stimulate one another to love and good deeds, not forsaking our own assembling together, as is the habit of some, but encouraging one another; and all the more as you see the day drawing near." This passage highlights the role of the church community in encouraging and edifying one another.

The Bible and Society

The principles and teachings of the Bible extend beyond individual and communal life to impact broader society. The Bible provides a moral and ethical framework that promotes justice, compassion, and righteousness.

IS THE BIBLE REALLY THE WORD OF GOD?

Justice and Righteousness

Micah 6:8 again serves as a key verse, emphasizing the call to do justice, love kindness, and walk humbly with God. These principles are foundational for building a just and compassionate society.

Compassion for the Vulnerable

The Bible repeatedly calls for care and compassion for the vulnerable, including widows, orphans, and the poor. James 1:27 underscores this, "Pure and undefiled religion in the sight of our God and Father is this: to visit orphans and widows in their distress, and to keep oneself unstained by the world." This call to social responsibility reflects the heart of God for the marginalized and oppressed.

Ethical Governance

Proverbs 29:2 states, "When the righteous increase, the people rejoice, but when a wicked man rules, people groan." This proverb highlights the importance of righteous leadership and ethical governance. The Bible provides principles that can guide leaders in making just and compassionate decisions for the welfare of society.

The Bible and Education

The Bible also plays a significant role in education, providing a foundation for knowledge, wisdom, and understanding.

The Source of Wisdom

Proverbs 1:7 declares, "The fear of Jehovah is the beginning of knowledge; fools despise wisdom and instruction." This verse underscores the importance of a reverent relationship with God as the foundation for true wisdom and knowledge.

Teaching and Learning

Deuteronomy 6:6-7 instructs, "These words, which I am commanding you today, shall be on your heart. You shall teach them diligently to your sons and shall talk of them when you sit in your house and when you walk by the way and when you lie down and when you rise up." This passage highlights the importance of teaching God's Word to the next generation, ensuring that His truths are passed down and applied in every aspect of life.

Integration of Faith and Learning

Colossians 2:3 states, "in whom are hidden all the treasures of wisdom and knowledge." This verse emphasizes that all true wisdom and knowledge are found in Christ. The integration of faith and learning ensures that education is rooted in the truth of God's Word, providing a holistic understanding of the world and our place in it.

The Enduring Relevance of the Bible

The Bible's teachings are not confined to a particular time or culture but are eternally relevant. Its principles continue to guide, inspire, and transform lives across generations and cultures.

Eternal Word

Isaiah 40:8 declares, "The grass withers, the flower fades, but the word of our God stands forever." This verse emphasizes the enduring nature of God's Word, assuring us that its truths remain relevant and authoritative across all ages.

Continual Application

Psalm 119:89 states, "Forever, O Jehovah, Your word is settled in heaven." The eternal nature of God's Word means that its teachings and principles are continually applicable, providing timeless guidance for every generation.

Transcultural Impact

The Bible's impact is not limited by cultural or geographical boundaries. Its message of hope, redemption, and transformation resonates with people from diverse backgrounds and cultures, demonstrating its universal relevance and power.

The Personal Invitation

Ultimately, the Bible extends a personal invitation to every individual to enter into a relationship with God, grow in faith, and live out His purposes.

Invitation to Salvation

Revelation 3:20 presents a personal invitation from Jesus, "Behold, I stand at the door and knock; if anyone hears My voice and opens the door, I will come in to him and will dine with him, and he with Me." This invitation to salvation and fellowship with Christ is extended to all who believe and respond in faith.

Call to Discipleship

Matthew 16:24-25 records Jesus' call to discipleship, "Then Jesus said to His disciples, 'If anyone wishes to come after Me, he must deny himself, and take up his cross and follow Me. For whoever wishes to save his life will lose it; but whoever loses his life for My sake will find it.'" This call to follow Jesus involves a commitment to live according to His teachings and to participate in His mission.

Promise of Eternal Life

John 10:27-28 provides the assurance of eternal life for those who follow Jesus, "My sheep hear My voice, and I know them, and they follow Me; and I give eternal life to them, and they will never perish; and no one will snatch them out of My hand." This promise of eternal life and security in Christ is a central aspect of the Bible's message and relevance.

The Bible's profound impact on individual lives, communities, and societies demonstrates its living and active nature. Its divine inspiration, practical guidance, and enduring relevance make it a vital resource for believers, offering wisdom, encouragement, and hope for every aspect of life.

Edward D. Andrews

SECTION 2 EMBATTLED CHRISTIANITY

CHAPTER 18 Christianity—Was Jesus the Way to God?

The Exclusivity of Christ's Claim

Jesus Christ made a bold and exclusive claim about His role as the way to God. In John 14:6, Jesus declares, "I am the way, and the truth, and the life; no one comes to the Father but through Me." This statement underscores the uniqueness of Jesus' position as the only path to reconciliation with God. It affirms that Jesus is not merely one way among many, but the definitive and only way to the Father.

The Fulfillment of Prophecy

The Old Testament is replete with prophecies pointing to the coming Messiah, all of which find their fulfillment in Jesus Christ. Isaiah 53:5, written around 700 B.C.E., foretells the suffering servant who would bear the sins of many: "But He was pierced through for our transgressions, He was crushed for our iniquities; the chastening for our well-being fell upon Him, and by His scourging we are healed." This prophecy, among many others, was fulfilled in the person of Jesus, validating His claim as the promised Savior.

The Testimony of John the Baptist

John the Baptist, a pivotal figure in the New Testament, identified Jesus as the Lamb of God who takes away the sin of the world. In John 1:29, John the Baptist proclaims, "Behold, the Lamb of God who takes away the sin of the world!" This recognition of Jesus as the sacrificial Lamb echoes the Old Testament sacrificial system and highlights Jesus' role in providing atonement for sin.

Jesus' Miracles as Evidence

The miracles performed by Jesus serve as powerful evidence of His divine authority and identity. These miracles, ranging from healing the sick to raising the dead, authenticate His claims and demonstrate His power over nature, disease, and death.

Healing the Blind Man

In John 9, Jesus heals a man born blind, a miracle that astonishes the witnesses and leads to a profound confession of faith. John 9:32-33 records the healed man's response to the Pharisees, "Since the beginning of time it has never been heard that anyone opened the eyes of a person born blind. If this man were not from God, He could do nothing." This miracle not only demonstrates Jesus' power but also His compassion and willingness to restore those who are marginalized.

Raising Lazarus from the Dead

One of the most significant miracles recorded in the Gospels is the raising of Lazarus from the dead. In John 11:25-26, Jesus declares to Martha, "I am the resurrection and the life; he who believes in Me will live even if he dies, and everyone who lives and believes in Me will never die. Do you believe this?" This miracle, culminating in Lazarus walking out of the tomb after four days, powerfully affirms Jesus' authority over life and death and His promise of eternal life to those who believe in Him.

The Teaching of Jesus

Jesus' teachings further solidify His claim as the way to God. His Sermon on the Mount, recorded in Matthew 5-7, presents a radical and profound vision of God's kingdom, emphasizing righteousness, mercy, and love. These teachings challenge conventional wisdom and call for a transformative way of living that reflects God's character.

The Beatitudes

The Beatitudes, found in Matthew 5:3-12, outline the characteristics of those who belong to God's kingdom. Jesus begins with, "Blessed are the poor in spirit, for theirs is the kingdom of heaven." These statements highlight the values of humility, mercy, and purity, setting a high moral standard that points to the need for God's grace and the transformative power of the Holy Spirit.

The Great Commandment

Jesus encapsulates the essence of the Law and the Prophets in the Great Commandment. In Matthew 22:37-40, Jesus declares, "You shall love Jehovah your God with all your heart, and with all your soul, and with all your mind. This is the great and foremost commandment. The second is like it, You shall love your neighbor as yourself. On these two commandments depend the whole Law and the Prophets." This commandment underscores the centrality of love in the Christian life, both towards God and others.

The Death and Resurrection of Jesus

The death and resurrection of Jesus are the cornerstone of the Christian faith, providing the ultimate proof of His claim as the way to God. These events demonstrate God's love and justice, offering forgiveness and eternal life to all who believe.

The Atoning Sacrifice

Jesus' death on the cross serves as the atoning sacrifice for sin, fulfilling the sacrificial system established in the Old Testament. In 1 John 2:2, it is written, "And He Himself is the propitiation for our sins; and not for ours only, but also for those of the whole world." This sacrificial death provides the means for reconciliation with God, satisfying His justice and demonstrating His love.

The Resurrection

The resurrection of Jesus is the definitive proof of His divine identity and the validation of His claims. In 1 Corinthians 15:3-4, Paul emphasizes the importance of the resurrection, "For I delivered to you as of first importance what I also received, that Christ died for our sins according to the Scriptures, and that He was buried, and that He was raised on the third day according to the Scriptures." The resurrection not only affirms Jesus' victory over sin and death but also assures believers of their future resurrection and eternal life with God.

The Apostolic Witness

The apostles, eyewitnesses of Jesus' life, death, and resurrection, provide a compelling testimony to His identity and mission. Their transformed lives and willingness to suffer and die for their faith underscore the truth of their message.

Peter's Confession

Peter's confession in Matthew 16:16 is a pivotal moment in the Gospels: "Simon Peter answered, 'You are the Christ, the Son of the living God.'" This declaration affirms Jesus' identity as the Messiah and the Son of God, a truth revealed to Peter by the Father.

Paul's Testimony

The apostle Paul, once a persecutor of Christians, became one of the most ardent defenders of the faith after encountering the risen Christ. In Galatians 1:11-12, Paul asserts, "For I would have you know, brethren, that the gospel which was preached by me is not according to man. For I neither received it from man, nor was I taught it, but I received it through a revelation of Jesus Christ." Paul's transformation and his extensive missionary work provide powerful evidence of the truth of the Gospel.

The Witness of the Early Church

The early church, empowered by the Holy Spirit, spread the message of Jesus' resurrection and the way to God throughout the Roman Empire and beyond. Their communal life and testimony continue to inspire believers today.

The Day of Pentecost

Acts 2 records the coming of the Holy Spirit on the Day of Pentecost, empowering the apostles to proclaim the Gospel boldly. Acts 2:4 states, "And they were all filled with the Holy Spirit and began to speak with other tongues, as the Spirit was giving them utterance." This event marks the beginning of the church's mission to spread the Gospel to all nations.

Communal Life

The early church exemplified a communal life marked by devotion to the apostles' teaching, fellowship, breaking of bread, and prayer. Acts 2:42 describes this life: "They were continually devoting themselves to the apostles' teaching and to fellowship, to the breaking of bread and to prayer." This community life, characterized by love and mutual support, provides a model for Christian fellowship today.

The Continued Impact of Jesus' Teachings

IS THE BIBLE REALLY THE WORD OF GOD?

The teachings of Jesus have continued to impact individuals and societies throughout history. His principles of love, justice, and forgiveness have inspired countless acts of charity, social reform, and personal transformation.

The Sermon on the Mount

The principles laid out in the Sermon on the Mount, such as turning the other cheek (Matthew 5:39) and loving one's enemies (Matthew 5:44), have challenged and transformed ethical thinking. These teachings call believers to a higher standard of love and righteousness, reflecting the character of God.

The Parable of the Good Samaritan

In the Parable of the Good Samaritan (Luke 10:30-37), Jesus teaches the importance of compassion and neighborly love. This parable has inspired countless acts of charity and social justice, highlighting the call to love and serve others regardless of social boundaries.

Jesus' Promise of Eternal Life

Central to Jesus' message is the promise of eternal life for those who believe in Him. This promise provides hope and assurance to believers, motivating them to live faithfully and to share the Gospel with others.

The Assurance of Salvation

John 10:28-29 provides assurance of eternal life: "and I give eternal life to them, and they will never perish; and no one will snatch them out of My hand. My Father, who has given them to Me, is greater than all; and no one is able to snatch them out of the Father's hand." This promise underscores the security and permanence of the salvation offered by Jesus.

The Promise of Heaven

In John 14:1-3, Jesus promises to prepare a place for His followers in heaven: "Do not let your heart be troubled; believe in God, believe also in Me. In My Father's house are many dwelling places; if it were not so, I would have told you; for I go to prepare a place for you. If I go and prepare a place for you, I will come again and receive you to Myself, that where I am, there you may be also." This promise of eternal fellowship with God provides hope and comfort to believers.

The Transforming Power of the Gospel

The Gospel of Jesus Christ continues to transform lives today, offering forgiveness, hope, and a new beginning. The transformative power of the Gospel is evidenced in the countless testimonies of individuals who have experienced radical change through faith in Jesus.

New Creation in Christ

2 Corinthians 5:17 declares, "Therefore if anyone is in Christ, he is a new creature; the old things passed away; behold, new things have come." This verse highlights the profound transformation that occurs when a person places their faith in Jesus, becoming a new creation with a renewed purpose and identity.

Freedom from Sin

Romans 6:22-23 describes the freedom from sin that believers experience through Christ: "But now having been freed from sin and enslaved to God, you derive your benefit, resulting in sanctification, and the outcome, eternal life. For the wages of sin is death, but the free gift of God is eternal life in Christ Jesus our Lord." This freedom from sin and the gift of eternal life are central to the transformative power of the Gospel.

The Global Reach of Christianity

The message of Jesus as the way to God has spread across the globe, impacting diverse cultures and societies. Christianity's global reach testifies to the universal relevance and transformative power of the Gospel.

The Great Commission

Jesus' final instruction to His disciples, known as the Great Commission, emphasizes the global scope of the Gospel mission. In Matthew 28:19-20, Jesus commands, "Go therefore and make disciples of all the nations, baptizing them in the name of the Father and the Son and the Holy Spirit, teaching them to observe all that I commanded you; and lo, I am with you always, even to the end of the age." This commission underscores the call to share the message of Jesus with all nations.

Growth of the Church

The rapid growth of the early church, as recorded in the book of Acts, demonstrates the compelling nature of the Gospel message. Acts 2:41 reports, "So then, those who had received his word were baptized; and that day there were added about three thousand souls." This growth continues today, as millions around the world embrace the message of Jesus and experience the transformative power of the Gospel.

The Future Hope

The Bible promises a future hope for all who trust in Jesus, including the return of Christ, the resurrection of the dead, and the establishment of God's eternal kingdom.

The Return of Christ

Jesus promised to return and establish His kingdom. Revelation 22:12 records Jesus' words, "Behold, I am coming quickly, and My reward is with Me, to render to every man according to what he has done." This promise of Jesus' return provides hope and encouragement to believers, motivating them to live faithfully and anticipate His coming.

The Resurrection of the Dead

The promise of the resurrection is a cornerstone of Christian hope. 1 Thessalonians 4:16-17 states, "For the Lord Himself will descend from heaven with a shout, with the voice of the archangel and with the trumpet of God, and the dead in Christ will rise first. Then we who are alive and remain will be caught up together with them in the clouds to meet the Lord in the air, and so we shall always be with the Lord." This assurance of resurrection and eternal life provides comfort and hope to believers.

The New Heaven and New Earth

The Bible concludes with the vision of a new heaven and new earth, where God will dwell with His people forever. Revelation 21:1-

4 describes this future hope: "Then I saw a new heaven and a new earth; for the first heaven and the first earth passed away, and there is no longer any sea. And I saw the holy city, new Jerusalem, coming down out of heaven from God, made ready as a bride adorned for her husband. And I heard a loud voice from the throne, saying, 'Behold, the tabernacle of God is among men, and He will dwell among them, and they shall be His people, and God Himself will be among them, and He will wipe away every tear from their eyes; and there will no longer be any death; there will no longer be any mourning, or crying, or pain; the first things have passed away.'" This vision of eternal fellowship with God provides the ultimate hope and motivation for believers.

The evidence from Scripture, the testimony of the apostles, the transformative power of the Gospel, and the global impact of Christianity all affirm that Jesus is indeed the way to God. His unique claim, backed by His fulfillment of prophecy, miracles, teachings, death, and resurrection, provides a compelling case for His role as the exclusive path to reconciliation with God.

CHAPTER 19 Why Are There So Many Christian Denominations?

The Great Apostasy Develops

"ONE Lord, one faith." (Ephesians 4:5) When the apostle Paul penned those words around 60-61 C.E., there was but one Christian faith. Today, however, we see a myriad of denominations, sects, and cults that claim to be Christian, yet teach conflicting doctrines and hold different standards of conduct. This divergence from the unified Christian congregation that began on Pentecost 33 C.E. prompts us to ask: How did these divisions come about?

From the very beginning, Satan tried to silence the testimony of the Christian witnesses of Jehovah by bringing upon them persecution from those outside the congregation. (1 Peter 5:8) Initially, this persecution came from the Jews and then from the Gentile Roman Empire. Despite enduring all manner of opposition, the early Christians remained steadfast. (Compare Revelation 1:9; 2:3, 19.) However, the Adversary did not relent. If external pressure could not silence the Christians, he aimed to corrupt them from within. Even in its infancy, the Christian congregation faced the threat of internal apostasy.

"There Will . . . Be False Teachers Among You"

Jesus warned His followers about the inevitable rise of false teachers. "Be on the watch," He cautioned, "for the false prophets that come to you in sheep's covering." (Matthew 7:15) Jesus knew Satan would try to divide and corrupt His followers, so He warned them early in His ministry about false teachers.

The apostle Paul, around 56 C.E., warned the overseers of Ephesus that "from among you yourselves" men would arise, speaking twisted things to draw away disciples after themselves. (Acts 20:29, 30) These apostates would not be content with merely having their own followers; they would endeavor to draw away Christ's disciples. The apostle Peter, around 64 C.E., also foretold internal corruption, describing false teachers who would "quietly bring in destructive sects" and exploit believers with counterfeit words. (2 Peter 2:1, 3)

"Already at Work"

Less than 20 years after Jesus' death, the apostle Paul indicated that Satan's efforts to cause division and turn men away from the true faith were "already at work." (2 Thessalonians 2:7) By around 49 C.E., the church leaders in Jerusalem noted that some from among the congregation were causing trouble with their speeches, despite having no instructions to do so. (Acts 15:24) This opposition was evident in the controversy over whether Gentile Christians needed to be circumcised and observe the Mosaic Law. (Acts 15:1, 5)

As the first century progressed, divisive thinking spread. By around 51 C.E., some in Thessalonica wrongly predicted that the presence of the Lord Jesus was imminent. (2 Thessalonians 2:1, 2) By around 55 C.E., some in Corinth rejected the clear Christian teaching regarding the resurrection of the dead. (1 Corinthians 15:12) By around 65 C.E., others claimed that the resurrection had already taken place in a symbolic form. (2 Timothy 2:16-18)

By the time the apostle John wrote his letters around 98 C.E., there were "many antichrists" who denied that "Jesus is the Christ" and that Jesus is the Son of God who came "in the flesh." (1 John 2:18, 22; 4:2, 3) For over 60 years, the apostles had acted as a restraint against the tide of apostasy. (2 Thessalonians 2:7) However, as the last surviving apostle, John, died around 100 C.E., the apostasy that had slowly begun to creep into the congregation was ready to burst forth unrestrained, leading to significant organizational and doctrinal changes.

The Rise of Clergy and Laity

Jesus taught His disciples that "all you are brothers" and that "your Leader is one, the Christ." (Matthew 23:8, 10) In the first century, there was no clergy class within Christian congregations. All early Christians, as spirit-anointed brothers of Christ, had the prospect of being heavenly priests with Him. (1 Peter 1:3, 4; 2:5, 9) Each congregation was supervised by a body of overseers or spiritual elders, who all had equal authority and were not to lord it over the flock. (Acts 20:17; Philippians 1:1; 1 Peter 5:2, 3)

However, as apostasy unfolded, changes occurred quickly. One of the earliest deviations was the separation between the terms "overseer" (episkopos) and "older man" or "elder" (presbyteros), which were no longer used interchangeably. Just a decade or so after the death of the apostle John, Ignatius, the "bishop" of Antioch, wrote advocating for each congregation to be supervised by one bishop who was distinct from and had greater authority than the presbyters.

By the second century, a standing office of president of the presbyters had formed, to whom the name episkopos was given. This individual was distinguished from the rest of the presbyters, laying the groundwork for a clergy class. About a century later, Cyprian, the "bishop" of Carthage, was a strong advocate of the bishops' authority as a group separate from the presbyters (later known as priests), deacons, and laity.

The Council of Nicaea and Beyond

By the time of the Council of Nicaea in 325 C.E., significant divisions and theological disputes had already taken root within the church. The Council of Nicaea addressed the Arian controversy, which questioned the divinity of Christ. The Nicene Creed affirmed the belief in Jesus Christ as "begotten, not made, being of one substance with the Father." This creed aimed to unify Christian doctrine but also highlighted existing divisions.

Following the Council of Nicaea, further councils and debates continued to address theological issues and schisms. The Council of Chalcedon in 451 C.E. produced the Chalcedonian Definition, affirming that Jesus is fully God and fully man, existing in two natures without confusion or separation. This definition, while crucial for orthodox Christology, led to further schisms, with some groups rejecting the Chalcedonian formulation.

The Great Schism of 1054

The Great Schism of 1054 resulted in the separation of the Western (Roman Catholic) and Eastern (Orthodox) churches. This schism was caused by theological, political, and cultural factors, including the Filioque clause, which was added to the Nicene Creed by the Western church and stated that the Holy Spirit proceeds from the Father and the Son. The Eastern church maintained that the Holy Spirit proceeds from the Father alone, highlighting deeper theological divergences.

Politically, the division of the Roman Empire into Eastern and Western halves created distinct cultural and administrative centers. The Western church, centered in Rome, developed its own traditions and practices, while the Eastern church, centered in Constantinople, developed differently. These cultural and political differences exacerbated theological disputes, leading to mutual excommunications in 1054.

The Protestant Reformation

The Protestant Reformation in the 16th century marked another significant division within Christianity. Initiated by figures like Martin Luther, John Calvin, and Ulrich Zwingli, the Reformation sought to reform the Roman Catholic Church but ultimately led to the creation of new denominations.

Martin Luther and the Ninety-Five Theses

Martin Luther's posting of the Ninety-Five Theses in 1517 challenged the Roman Catholic Church's teachings on indulgences, salvation, and the authority of the pope. Luther's emphasis on salvation by faith alone (sola fide) and the authority of Scripture alone (sola scriptura) became foundational principles for Protestant theology.

John Calvin and Reformed Theology

John Calvin developed a comprehensive theological system known as Reformed theology, emphasizing predestination and the sovereignty of God. Calvin's teachings influenced the formation of various Reformed denominations, further diversifying the Christian landscape.

Post-Reformation Denominations

The aftermath of the Protestant Reformation saw the emergence of numerous denominations, each with distinct beliefs and practices. Some of the key denominations include:

IS THE BIBLE REALLY THE WORD OF GOD?

The Lutheran Church

The Lutheran Church, founded by Martin Luther, emphasized justification by faith alone and the authority of Scripture. It retained some liturgical elements of the Roman Catholic Church while rejecting its doctrinal errors.

The Reformed Churches

The Reformed Churches, influenced by John Calvin and Ulrich Zwingli, emphasized the sovereignty of God, predestination, and a simpler form of worship. These churches include the Presbyterian and Congregationalist traditions.

The Anglican Church

The Anglican Church, established by King Henry VIII, sought to maintain a middle way between Roman Catholicism and Protestantism. It retained many liturgical practices of the Catholic Church while embracing Reformation principles.

The Anabaptists

The Anabaptists, a radical Reformation movement, emphasized believer's baptism, separation from the state, and a commitment to pacifism. Their descendants include the Mennonites and Amish.

Modern Denominational Landscape

The modern Christian landscape is characterized by a multitude of denominations, each with unique theological emphases, worship styles, and organizational structures. These denominations can be broadly categorized into several traditions:

Evangelicalism

Evangelicalism emphasizes the authority of Scripture, personal conversion, and evangelism. It encompasses a wide range of denominations, including Baptists, Pentecostals, and non-denominational churches.

Pentecostalism

Pentecostalism, which emerged in the early 20th century, emphasizes the work of the Holy Spirit, spiritual gifts, and experiential worship. It includes denominations like the Assemblies of God and the Church of God in Christ.

Mainline Protestantism

Mainline Protestant denominations, such as the United Methodist Church, the Episcopal Church, and the Evangelical Lutheran Church in America, tend to emphasize social justice, liturgical worship, and a more liberal theological perspective.

Orthodox Christianity

The Eastern Orthodox Church and the Oriental Orthodox Churches maintain ancient liturgical traditions and emphasize the continuity of apostolic succession and the importance of the ecumenical councils.

Roman Catholicism

Roman Catholicism, with its hierarchical structure and emphasis on the sacraments, remains one of the largest Christian traditions. It acknowledges the pope as the spiritual leader and upholds doctrines such as transubstantiation and the veneration of saints.

The Role of Theological Interpretation and Cultural Context

The proliferation of denominations can also be attributed to differences in theological interpretation and cultural context. Theological debates over issues such as baptism, communion, predestination, and church governance have led to the formation of distinct denominational identities.

Baptism and Communion

Debates over the mode and meaning of baptism and the nature of communion have been central to denominational differences. Some denominations practice infant baptism, while others emphasize believer's baptism. Similarly, views on the presence of Christ in communion vary from transubstantiation to symbolic memorialism.

Predestination and Free Will

Theological perspectives on predestination and free will have also divided denominations. Calvinist traditions emphasize God's sovereignty and predestination, while Arminian traditions uphold the importance of human free will and responsibility.

Church Governance

Differences in church governance, such as episcopal, presbyterian, and congregational systems, have further diversified the Christian landscape. Episcopal systems emphasize hierarchical leadership, presbyterian systems prioritize representative leadership, and congregational systems advocate for local church autonomy.

Cultural and Historical Contexts

Cultural and historical contexts have shaped denominational development. The Reformation, the Enlightenment, and the Great Awakenings, among other historical events, influenced theological and organizational changes within Christianity. Additionally, cultural factors, such as language, ethnicity, and regional traditions, have contributed to the formation of distinct denominational identities.

Conclusion

The existence of numerous Christian denominations is the result of a complex interplay of historical, theological, and cultural factors. From the early church's struggles with apostasy and doctrinal disputes to the Great Schism, the Protestant Reformation, and modern theological debates, these divisions reflect the diverse ways in which believers have sought to understand and live out their faith. There are Christian denominations that reflect biblical teachings and first century Christianity but almost all have strayed from true Christianity of the first century and the Word of God. However, even in those, there are true Christians searching for the truth. Like God set up first century Christianity replacing the Israelite religion, He can again before the Great Tribulation, or at Armageddon, help the true Christians in each denomination to survive through Armageddon.

Edward D. Andrews

CHAPTER 20 The Great Apostasy—The Way to God Blocked in the Middle Ages

The Early Warnings of Apostasy

From the very inception of the Christian church, warnings about the rise of apostasy were evident. Jesus Himself cautioned His followers: "Be on the watch for false prophets that come to you in sheep's covering." (Matthew 7:15) This was a clear indication that false teachings and teachers would infiltrate the Christian community, masquerading as genuine followers of Christ.

The Apostolic Era and Early Schisms

Even during the lifetime of the apostles, schisms and false teachings began to emerge. The apostle Paul, writing around 56 C.E., warned the Ephesian elders: "From among you yourselves men will rise and speak twisted things to draw away the disciples after themselves." (Acts 20:29-30) Paul's letters frequently addressed these internal threats. For instance, in his letter to the Galatians, he expressed astonishment that they were "so quickly deserting Him who called you by the grace of Christ, for a different gospel." (Galatians 1:6)

The Growth of Apostasy in the First Century

As the first century progressed, the seeds of apostasy began to take root more deeply. By about 49 C.E., some within the early church were causing confusion over the necessity of circumcision for Gentile converts, leading to the Jerusalem Council's decision to clarify this issue (Acts 15:1, 5, 24). By 51 C.E., some in Thessalonica were erroneously proclaiming that the day of the Lord had already come (2 Thessalonians 2:1-2). In Corinth, by around 55 C.E., some denied the resurrection of the dead (1 Corinthians 15:12), while others in Ephesus were propagating false doctrines about the resurrection having already occurred in a symbolic sense (2 Timothy 2:16-18).

Post-Apostolic Era and the Rise of Clergy

With the death of the last apostle, John, around 100 C.E., the early church lost its direct apostolic guidance, which had acted as a restraint against widespread apostasy (2 Thessalonians 2:7). This opened the door for significant organizational changes and the rise of a hierarchical structure within the church. Jesus had emphasized that all His followers were brothers and that only He was their Leader (Matthew 23:8, 10). However, by the second century, a clear distinction between clergy and laity began to emerge.

The Separation of Clergy and Laity

Initially, terms like "overseer" (episkopos) and "elder" (presbyteros) were used interchangeably. However, by the early second century, these roles began to diverge. Ignatius of Antioch, writing around 110 C.E., advocated for a single bishop to oversee each congregation, distinguishing the bishop from the elders. He wrote: "Follow the bishop as Jesus Christ follows the Father, and the presbytery as if it were the Apostles." This marked the beginning of a hierarchical structure where bishops held more authority than the elders.

Development of Hierarchical Structure

By the second century, the office of the bishop became more prominent, with bishops presiding over the presbyters. This development laid the groundwork for a distinct clergy class. Cyprian, the bishop of Carthage in the mid-third century, was a strong proponent of episcopal authority, emphasizing the power of bishops as a separate class from the presbyters and laity. His views significantly influenced the development of a structured ecclesiastical hierarchy.

The Council of Nicaea and the Consolidation of Power

The Council of Nicaea in 325 C.E. was a pivotal moment in church history. Convened by Emperor Constantine, this council sought to address the Arian controversy, which questioned the divinity of Christ. The Nicene Creed, formulated at this council, affirmed the belief in Jesus Christ as "begotten, not made, being of one substance with the Father." While this creed aimed to unify Christian doctrine, it also highlighted existing divisions and further solidified the hierarchical structure of the church.

The Role of Constantine and State Involvement

The involvement of Emperor Constantine in the Council of Nicaea marked a significant shift in the relationship between the church and the state. Constantine's conversion to Christianity and his subsequent patronage of the church brought the Christian faith into a closer alignment with the Roman state. This alignment had profound implications, including the consolidation of ecclesiastical power and the establishment of Christianity as a state religion.

The Great Schism of 1054

The Great Schism of 1054 was a major event that further divided Christendom. This schism resulted in the separation of the Western (Roman Catholic) and Eastern (Orthodox) churches. Theological, political, and cultural differences fueled this split. One major theological issue was the Filioque clause, which the Western church added to the Nicene Creed. This clause stated that the Holy Spirit proceeds from the Father and the Son, whereas the Eastern church maintained that the Holy Spirit proceeds from the Father alone. This doctrinal disagreement, along with other theological and liturgical differences, led to mutual excommunications and the formal division of the church.

The Medieval Church and the Rise of Papal Power

During the Middle Ages, the Western church, centered in Rome, saw a significant increase in the power and influence of the papacy. The doctrine of papal supremacy, which held that the pope had supreme authority over the entire Christian church, became more entrenched. This period saw the development of the doctrine of the papacy and the consolidation of papal authority, culminating in declarations such as the Dictatus Papae in the 11th century, which asserted the pope's authority over secular rulers.

Corruption and Reform Movements

The medieval church was not immune to corruption. The sale of indulgences, simony (the buying and selling of ecclesiastical offices), and moral laxity among the clergy were rampant. These abuses led to various reform movements, both within and outside the official structures of the church.

The Waldensians and Albigensians

In the 12th and 13th centuries, groups like the Waldensians and Albigensians emerged, advocating for a return to apostolic poverty and a more personal, direct relationship with God. These movements were often brutally suppressed by the church, which viewed them as heretical threats to its authority.

The Inquisition

To combat heresy and enforce doctrinal conformity, the medieval church established the Inquisition. This institution used various means, including torture and execution, to root out heresy and maintain ecclesiastical authority. The Inquisition's actions often led to widespread fear and repression, further alienating many from the established church.

The Proto-Reformation and Pre-Reformers

Before the Protestant Reformation of the 16th century, several figures and movements laid the groundwork for reform.

John Wycliffe

John Wycliffe, an English theologian in the 14th century, criticized the church's wealth and corruption and translated the Bible into English, making it accessible to the common people. Wycliffe's followers, known as Lollards, faced persecution for their beliefs.

Jan Hus

Jan Hus, a Bohemian reformer influenced by Wycliffe, also called for church reform and greater access to the Scriptures. Hus was ultimately condemned as a heretic and burned at the stake in 1415. His martyrdom sparked the Hussite Wars and contributed to the growing desire for reform within the church.

The Protestant Reformation

The Protestant Reformation, initiated by Martin Luther in the early 16th century, was a response to the widespread corruption and doctrinal errors within the Roman Catholic Church. Luther's Ninety-Five Theses, posted in 1517, challenged the sale of indulgences and other practices, sparking a movement that would forever change the landscape of Christianity.

Martin Luther and Sola Scriptura

Luther's emphasis on sola scriptura (Scripture alone) and sola fide (faith alone) challenged the authority of the pope and the church's teachings. His translation of the Bible into German made the Scriptures accessible to the general populace, empowering individuals to read and interpret the Bible for themselves.

John Calvin and Reformed Theology

John Calvin, another key figure in the Reformation, developed a systematic theology that emphasized the sovereignty of God, predestination, and the priesthood of all believers. Calvin's teachings influenced the development of various Reformed denominations, further diversifying the Christian landscape.

The Anabaptists

The Anabaptists, a radical Reformation movement, advocated for believer's baptism, separation from the state, and a commitment to pacifism. Their emphasis on a voluntary church composed of true believers led to the formation of distinct communities, often facing severe persecution for their beliefs.

The Counter-Reformation

In response to the Protestant Reformation, the Roman Catholic Church initiated the Counter-Reformation, a period of significant reform and renewal. The Council of Trent (1545-1563) addressed doctrinal issues and sought to correct abuses within the church. While the Counter-Reformation reaffirmed many traditional Catholic doctrines, it also led to the establishment of new religious orders, such as the Jesuits, and a renewed emphasis on education and missionary work.

The Fragmentation of Christianity

The Reformation and Counter-Reformation periods saw the fragmentation of Christianity into numerous denominations and traditions. These divisions were often influenced by theological, political, and cultural factors, leading to the diverse Christian landscape we see today.

Conclusion

The Great Apostasy and subsequent historical developments led to significant organizational and doctrinal changes within Christianity. From the early warnings of apostasy by Jesus and the apostles to the medieval church's rise in hierarchical power and the Reformation's call for reform, the history of Christianity is marked by a continuous struggle to maintain doctrinal purity and organizational integrity. Despite these challenges, the central message of the Gospel remains unchanged, offering hope and salvation to all who believe.

Edward D. Andrews

CHAPTER 21 The Reformation—The Search for God

The State of the Church Pre-Reformation

By the late medieval period, the Christian church had undergone significant transformation from its early apostolic roots. The rise of a hierarchical clergy, the centralization of ecclesiastical power in the hands of the bishops, and particularly the bishop of Rome, led to widespread corruption and doctrinal deviations from the teachings of the early church. These changes laid the groundwork for a major upheaval that would come to be known as the Reformation.

Corruption and Abuse in the Medieval Church

The church of the medieval period was marked by a series of abuses that increasingly drew criticism and discontent from both laypeople and clergy who sought a return to biblical purity.

Indulgences and Simony

One of the most notorious practices was the sale of indulgences. Indulgences were believed to reduce the punishment for sins, and they were sold to raise money for church projects, such as the construction of St. Peter's Basilica in Rome. The selling of church offices (simony) and positions was another significant issue, as it allowed wealth and power to corrupt the spiritual leadership of the church.

Moral Laxity Among Clergy

The moral integrity of many clergy members was called into question. Numerous reports of priests and bishops leading lives of luxury, engaging in sexual immorality, and neglecting their spiritual duties caused widespread scandal and eroded the credibility of the church.

Early Calls for Reform

IS THE BIBLE REALLY THE WORD OF GOD?

Long before the Reformation ignited in the 16th century, there were voices within Christendom that called for reform and a return to the teachings of the Scriptures.

John Wycliffe

In the 14th century, John Wycliffe, an English theologian and professor at the University of Oxford, became one of the earliest reformers. Wycliffe criticized the wealth and power of the church, condemned the practice of indulgences, and advocated for the translation of the Bible into vernacular languages so that laypeople could read it themselves. Wycliffe's followers, known as Lollards, spread his teachings despite facing severe persecution.

Jan Hus

Jan Hus, a Bohemian reformer influenced by Wycliffe, also called for reform. He preached against the moral failings of the clergy and the selling of indulgences. Hus emphasized the authority of the Scriptures over the church hierarchy. His execution in 1415 for heresy sparked outrage and led to the Hussite Wars, which further set the stage for the broader Reformation movement.

Martin Luther and the Spark of the Reformation

The Reformation is often dated to October 31, 1517, when Martin Luther, a German monk and professor of theology, nailed his Ninety-Five Theses to the door of the Wittenberg Castle Church. Luther's theses were a response to the sale of indulgences and called for a debate on the practices and doctrines of the church.

Sola Scriptura and Sola Fide

Luther's teachings emphasized two key principles: sola scriptura (Scripture alone) and sola fide (faith alone). Sola scriptura asserted that the Bible is the ultimate authority in all matters of faith and practice, above church traditions and teachings. Sola fide emphasized that salvation is attained through faith in Jesus Christ alone, not through human works or the purchasing of indulgences.

The Diet of Worms

In 1521, Luther was summoned to the Diet of Worms, an imperial council, to recant his teachings. His refusal to do so, famously declaring, "Here I stand; I can do no other. God help me. Amen," led to his excommunication and condemnation as an outlaw. However, Luther's ideas continued to spread, fueled by the printing press and growing discontent with the church.

The Spread of Reformation Ideas

The Reformation quickly spread beyond Germany, with various reformers in different regions adopting and adapting Luther's ideas to their contexts.

John Calvin

In Switzerland, John Calvin became a prominent figure in the Reformation. Calvin's teachings, known as Reformed theology, emphasized the sovereignty of God, predestination, and the priesthood of all believers. His work, "Institutes of the Christian Religion," provided a comprehensive theological framework for the Reformation movement and influenced many other reformers.

Ulrich Zwingli

Ulrich Zwingli, a contemporary of Luther in Zurich, Switzerland, also played a key role in the Reformation. Zwingli emphasized the authority of Scripture and rejected practices not explicitly found in the Bible, such as the veneration of saints and the use of images in worship.

The Anabaptists

The Anabaptists, another significant group within the Reformation, advocated for adult baptism, rejecting infant baptism as unscriptural. They also emphasized a separation from worldly affairs and the establishment of a community of believers committed to living according to the teachings of Jesus.

The Counter-Reformation

In response to the spread of Protestantism, the Roman Catholic Church initiated the Counter-Reformation, a series of reforms aimed at addressing the issues raised by the reformers and reaffirming Catholic doctrine.

IS THE BIBLE REALLY THE WORD OF GOD?

The Council of Trent

The Council of Trent (1545-1563) was a central component of the Counter-Reformation. The council addressed abuses within the church, clarified Catholic doctrines, and took steps to improve the education and moral integrity of the clergy. While the Council of Trent reaffirmed many traditional Catholic teachings, it also made significant efforts to address corruption and improve pastoral care.

New Religious Orders

New religious orders, such as the Jesuits founded by Ignatius of Loyola, played a crucial role in the Counter-Reformation. The Jesuits focused on education, missionary work, and the defense of Catholic doctrine, significantly contributing to the renewal of the church and its global expansion.

Theological Debates and Doctrinal Differences

The Reformation brought about a variety of theological debates and doctrinal differences that contributed to the fragmentation of Christianity into numerous denominations.

The Doctrine of Justification

The doctrine of justification was a central issue during the Reformation. Luther's emphasis on justification by faith alone (sola fide) clashed with the Catholic teaching that faith and works together contribute to salvation. This theological debate highlighted the different understandings of grace, faith, and works within Christianity.

The Lord's Supper

Another significant theological debate concerned the nature of the Lord's Supper (Eucharist). Luther maintained the real presence of Christ in the Eucharist (consubstantiation), while Zwingli viewed it as a symbolic memorial. Calvin offered a mediating position, emphasizing a spiritual presence of Christ in the sacrament.

Church Authority and Governance

The Reformation also brought differing views on church authority and governance. Protestant reformers rejected the papal authority and the hierarchical structure of the Catholic Church, advocating for various forms of church governance. Some, like the Lutherans, retained a form of episcopal governance, while others, like the Reformed and Presbyterian traditions, established systems of church governance based on councils and assemblies.

The Impact on Society and Culture

The Reformation had profound effects not only on religious life but also on society and culture as a whole.

Education and Literacy

The emphasis on sola scriptura led to a renewed focus on education and literacy, as people were encouraged to read the Bible for themselves. Protestant reformers established schools and universities to educate clergy and laity, leading to increased literacy rates and the spread of knowledge.

Political and Social Changes

The Reformation also brought about significant political and social changes. The questioning of religious authority paralleled challenges to political authority, contributing to the rise of nation-states and the decline of feudalism. The principle of the priesthood of all believers promoted ideas of equality and individual responsibility, influencing democratic developments in Europe.

Art and Music

The Reformation influenced art and music, particularly in Protestant regions. The rejection of religious images by some reformers led to a focus on other forms of artistic expression, such as music and literature. Hymnody became an essential part of Protestant worship, with figures like Martin Luther composing hymns that are still sung today.

The Legacy of the Reformation

While the Reformation led to the fragmentation of Western Christianity into various denominations, it also revitalized the Christian faith by returning to the foundational principles of the Scriptures and emphasizing a personal relationship with God through faith in Jesus Christ.

IS THE BIBLE REALLY THE WORD OF GOD?

Continuing the Search for God

The Reformation was a profound moment in the history of Christianity, characterized by a renewed search for God and a return to the teachings of the Scriptures. This movement, despite its divisions, aimed to purify the church and bring believers back to the core truths of the Christian faith.

Biblical Authority

The emphasis on biblical authority (sola scriptura) remains a cornerstone of Protestant theology. The belief that the Bible is the ultimate authority in matters of faith and practice continues to guide Christians in their understanding of God's will and their daily lives.

Salvation by Faith Alone

The doctrine of salvation by faith alone (sola fide) underscores the central message of the Gospel: that salvation is a gift of God's grace, received through faith in Jesus Christ. This principle, championed by Luther and other reformers, remains foundational to evangelical Christianity.

The Reformation's Call for Personal Faith

The Reformation emphasized the importance of personal faith and a direct relationship with God. This call for personal faith challenged the institutionalized practices of the medieval church and encouraged individuals to seek God through the Scriptures and prayer.

The Priesthood of All Believers

The doctrine of the priesthood of all believers, articulated by Luther, affirmed that all Christians have direct access to God through Jesus Christ and do not require a human mediator. This principle democratized the Christian faith and empowered laypeople to take an active role in their spiritual lives.

The Role of the Holy Spirit

The reformers emphasized the role of the Holy Spirit in guiding believers into all truth. While rejecting the idea of the indwelling Holy Spirit as understood in charismatic movements, they affirmed that the

Holy Spirit works through the Scriptures to convict, teach, and comfort believers.

Evangelism and Missions

The Reformation's focus on the authority of Scripture and the centrality of the Gospel also led to a renewed emphasis on evangelism and missions. The desire to share the message of salvation through faith in Jesus Christ has driven Protestant missions efforts around the world, leading to the spread of Christianity to new regions and cultures.

Conclusion

The Reformation was a pivotal event in the history of Christianity that sought to address the corruption and doctrinal errors of the medieval church. Through the efforts of reformers like Martin Luther, John Calvin, and others, the Reformation emphasized the authority of Scripture, salvation by faith alone, and the priesthood of all believers. These principles continue to shape evangelical Christianity today, guiding believers in their search for God and their commitment to living according to His Word.

CHAPTER 22 Modern Disbelief–Liberal to Moderate Christianity

The Rise of Liberal Theology

Liberal theology, emerging in the 19th century, sought to reconcile Christianity with modern science, philosophy, and cultural trends. It attempted to adapt Christian doctrines to contemporary thought, often at the expense of biblical authority and traditional beliefs. This movement emphasized human reason and experience over divine revelation, leading to significant shifts in theological perspectives.

The Historical-Critical Method

One of the hallmarks of liberal theology is the adoption of the historical-critical method of biblical interpretation. This approach scrutinizes the Bible using the same critical methods applied to other ancient texts, often questioning the historicity and supernatural elements of Scripture. By treating the Bible merely as a historical document, liberal theologians undermine its divine inspiration and authority. As 2 Timothy 3:16 states, "All Scripture is inspired by God and profitable for teaching, for reproof, for correction, for training in righteousness."

Rejection of Miracles and Supernatural Events

Liberal theologians often reject the miraculous and supernatural aspects of the Bible, viewing them as mythological or symbolic rather than literal events. This skepticism extends to the core tenets of the Christian faith, such as the virgin birth, resurrection, and miracles of Jesus. By denying these foundational truths, liberal theology strays far from the apostolic witness and the historical faith of the church. The resurrection of Jesus, for example, is a cornerstone of Christian belief, as Paul emphasizes in 1 Corinthians 15:14: "If Christ has not been raised, then our preaching is in vain, and your faith is in vain."

The Impact of Modernism on Christianity

Modernism, a cultural and intellectual movement that emerged in the late 19th and early 20th centuries, further influenced liberal theology. Modernism emphasized human progress, scientific advancement, and rationalism, often viewing traditional religious beliefs as outdated.

The Social Gospel Movement

The Social Gospel movement, influenced by modernist thought, emphasized social justice and ethical behavior over doctrinal purity. While addressing social issues such as poverty and inequality is important, the movement often neglected the necessity of personal salvation through faith in Jesus Christ. James 2:17 reminds us, "Even so faith, if it has no works, is dead, being by itself," emphasizing the balance of faith and works rather than substituting one for the other.

The De-emphasis on Doctrine

Modernist influence led to a de-emphasis on doctrinal teaching in favor of ethical living and social action. This shift often resulted in a dilution of the gospel message, focusing more on moralism than the redemptive work of Christ. Jesus' Great Commission in Matthew 28:19-20 instructs His followers to "make disciples of all nations, baptizing them in the name of the Father and the Son and the Holy Spirit, teaching them to observe all that I commanded you." This command underscores the importance of doctrinal teaching alongside ethical living.

The Rise of Progressive Christianity

In recent years, progressive Christianity has emerged, further diverging from traditional biblical teachings. This movement often embraces a relativistic approach to truth and morality, aligning itself with contemporary cultural values rather than Scripture.

Relativism and Moral Subjectivism

Progressive Christianity frequently adopts a relativistic view of truth, suggesting that moral and theological truths are not absolute but are subject to individual interpretation and cultural context. This perspective directly contradicts the biblical assertion of absolute truth, as Jesus declares in John 14:6, "I am the way, and the truth, and the life; no one comes to the Father but through Me."

Inclusivity and Affirmation

While inclusivity and compassion are important Christian virtues, progressive Christianity often extends these concepts to affirm lifestyles and behaviors that Scripture clearly defines as sinful. Romans 1:26-27 speaks against practices that deviate from God's design for human sexuality, yet progressive theology often reinterprets or ignores such passages to align with modern cultural norms.

Theological Drift in Moderate Christianity

Moderate Christianity, while not as radical as liberal or progressive strands, often exhibits a tendency to compromise on key doctrinal issues in an effort to remain culturally relevant and appealing.

The Quest for Relevance

In seeking to be relevant, many moderate churches downplay or avoid discussing controversial or challenging doctrines. This quest for relevance can lead to a watered-down gospel that lacks the transformative power of the full message of Christ. Paul warns Timothy in 2 Timothy 4:3-4, "For the time will come when they will not endure sound doctrine; but wanting to have their ears tickled, they will accumulate for themselves teachers in accordance to their own desires, and will turn away their ears from the truth and will turn aside to myths."

Compromise on Biblical Authority

Moderate Christianity often exhibits a flexible approach to biblical authority, treating certain biblical teachings as negotiable or culturally bound. This compromises the integrity of Scripture, which is described as "living and active and sharper than any two-edged sword" (Hebrews 4:12). The Word of God must be upheld as the ultimate authority in all matters of faith and practice.

The Consequences of Theological Compromise

The drift towards liberal, progressive, and moderate theologies has significant consequences for the church and individual believers.

Erosion of Doctrinal Clarity

As churches adopt these theologies, doctrinal clarity is often lost, leading to confusion and a lack of a firm foundation in the faith. Hosea 4:6 warns, "My people are destroyed for lack of knowledge." Without a clear understanding of biblical truth, believers are susceptible to false teachings and spiritual deception.

Moral and Ethical Relativism

The embrace of relativistic ethics undermines the moral authority of the church. When the church fails to stand firm on biblical principles, it loses its prophetic voice and ability to speak truth into society. Isaiah 5:20 declares, "Woe to those who call evil good, and good evil; Who substitute darkness for light and light for darkness; Who substitute bitter for sweet and sweet for bitter!"

Weakened Evangelistic Witness

A compromised gospel weakens the church's evangelistic witness. When the distinctiveness of the Christian message is blurred, the church loses its power to transform lives and draw people to Christ. Jesus called His followers to be "the salt of the earth" and "the light of the world" (Matthew 5:13-14). This call to distinctiveness is essential for effective evangelism.

The Call to Return to Biblical Christianity

In response to the challenges posed by modern disbelief, the church is called to return to the foundational truths of biblical Christianity.

Affirming Biblical Authority

A return to the authority of Scripture is paramount. The Bible must be upheld as the inspired and inerrant Word of God, guiding all aspects of faith and practice. Psalm 119:105 states, "Your word is a lamp to my feet and a light to my path." Embracing the full counsel of Scripture ensures that believers are grounded in truth.

Emphasizing Sound Doctrine

The church must prioritize sound doctrine, teaching and upholding the core tenets of the Christian faith. Paul instructed Titus to "speak the things which are fitting for sound doctrine" (Titus 2:1). Sound teaching equips believers to discern truth from error and to live lives that honor God.

Proclaiming the Gospel Boldly

The church must boldly proclaim the gospel of Jesus Christ, emphasizing salvation by grace through faith in Him alone. Romans 1:16 declares, "For I am not ashamed of the gospel, for it is the power of God for salvation to everyone who believes." The transformative power of the gospel must be central to the church's mission.

Living Counter-Culturally

Believers are called to live counter-culturally, upholding biblical values even when they conflict with societal norms. Romans 12:2 exhorts, "And do not be conformed to this world, but be transformed by the renewing of your mind, so that you may prove what the will of God is, that which is good and acceptable and perfect." Living distinctively as followers of Christ serves as a powerful testimony to the truth of the gospel.

Conclusion

The rise of liberal, progressive, and moderate theologies presents significant challenges to the Christian faith. By rejecting biblical authority, embracing relativism, and compromising on core doctrines, these movements undermine the foundation of Christianity. In response, the church is called to reaffirm its commitment to the authority of Scripture, sound doctrine, and the transformative power of the gospel. Only by returning to these foundational truths can the church effectively fulfill its mission and stand firm against the tide of modern disbelief.

Edward D. Andrews

CHAPTER 23 The Battle for the Bible— A Return to the True God

The False Dichotomy: The Bible vs. Science

In the late 1800s, a significant conflict began to surface between the realms of science and religion, often framed as a dichotomy between the Bible and scientific discovery. This period saw the rise of Darwinian evolution and the increasing influence of naturalism, which fundamentally challenged the biblical account of creation. Conservative evangelical Christian apologists have been at the forefront of defending the integrity and authority of the Bible against these scientific claims.

The Biblical Account of Creation

The Bible begins with a clear and definitive statement about the origin of the universe: "In the beginning God created the heavens and the earth" (Genesis 1:1). This declaration stands in contrast to the theory of evolution, which posits that life emerged through random processes over millions of years. While scientific discoveries have provided insight into the mechanisms of the natural world, they do not negate the fundamental truth that God is the Creator of all things. Hebrews 11:3 affirms, "By faith we understand that the worlds were prepared by the word of God, so that what is seen was not made out of things which are visible."

The Fixity of Kinds

The Bible teaches the fixity of kinds, indicating that God created distinct species that reproduce according to their kinds. Genesis 1:24-25 states, "Then God said, 'Let the earth bring forth living creatures after their kind: cattle and creeping things and beasts of the earth after their kind'; and it was so. God made the beasts of the earth after their kind, and the cattle after their kind, and everything that creeps on the ground after its kind; and God saw that it was good." This biblical principle stands in opposition to the evolutionary idea that all life forms share a common ancestor and have evolved over time through natural selection.

Astronomy and the Bible

The Bible also contains profound insights into the nature of the universe, long before modern science discovered these truths. For instance, Genesis 22:17 and Jeremiah 33:22 speak of the innumerable stars in the heavens, reflecting the vastness of the cosmos. The Bible's accuracy in these matters underscores its divine inspiration and reliability.

The Earth's Position and Structure

The Bible describes the earth's position and structure with remarkable accuracy. Isaiah 40:22 mentions "the circle of the earth," indicating its round shape. Job 26:7 states, "He stretches out the north over empty space and hangs the earth on nothing," accurately portraying the earth suspended in space. These descriptions align with modern scientific understanding, demonstrating the Bible's advanced knowledge.

Higher Criticism and Its Challenges

Higher criticism, also known as historical-critical methodology, emerged in the 19th century as scholars began applying critical methods to the study of the Bible. This approach often questioned the authorship, dating, and historical reliability of biblical texts, leading to widespread skepticism about the Bible's divine origin and authority.

Questioning Authorship and Dating

Higher critics frequently challenge the traditional authorship and dating of biblical books. For example, they question whether Moses wrote the Pentateuch or if the prophetic books were written by the prophets to whom they are attributed. Such skepticism undermines the historical and theological integrity of the Bible. However, Jesus Himself affirmed the Mosaic authorship of the Pentateuch (John 5:46-47) and the prophetic nature of the Old Testament (Luke 24:44).

The Documentary Hypothesis

One of the key theories in higher criticism is the Documentary Hypothesis, which posits that the Pentateuch is a compilation of multiple sources rather than the work of a single author, Moses. This theory divides the text into different strands, labeled J, E, D, and P, based on supposed differences in language and style. However, this hypothesis has been increasingly challenged by conservative scholars who argue for the unity and coherence of the Pentateuch as a divinely inspired work.

Abandonment of Literal Bible Translation

Another significant issue has been the shift away from literal Bible translation towards more dynamic or paraphrased translations. While dynamic translations aim to make the text more accessible, they often do so at the expense of accuracy and the original meaning.

The Importance of Literal Translation

Literal Bible translations seek to preserve the exact words and phrases used in the original languages, maintaining the integrity and depth of the Scriptures. Proverbs 30:5 declares, "Every word of God is tested; He is a shield to those who take refuge in Him." Literal translations uphold the precision and authority of God's Word, ensuring that believers receive the full counsel of Scripture.

The Danger of Paraphrased Translations

Paraphrased translations, while easier to read, can introduce interpretive biases and obscure the true meaning of the text. They risk altering the message of Scripture to fit contemporary language and cultural norms, potentially leading to doctrinal misunderstandings. 2 Timothy 2:15 urges believers to "accurately handle the word of truth," highlighting the necessity of careful and faithful translation.

Textual Scholars and the Quest for the Original Text

Textual criticism is a field dedicated to studying the manuscripts of the Bible to determine the most accurate representation of the original text. However, there has been a concerning trend among some textual scholars to move away from this primary goal.

IS THE BIBLE REALLY THE WORD OF GOD?

The Primacy of the Original Text

The original autographs of the biblical texts are divinely inspired and inerrant. Psalm 12:6 states, "The words of Jehovah are pure words; As silver tried in a furnace on the earth, refined seven times." Conservative textual critics focus on reconstructing the original text with the highest degree of accuracy, using the wealth of manuscript evidence available.

The Shift in Textual Criticism

Recently, some textual scholars have shifted their focus to understanding the history and transmission of the text rather than striving to ascertain the original wording. This shift can lead to a diminished confidence in the reliability of the Scriptures. The goal of textual criticism should remain the restoration of the original text, ensuring that believers have access to the true Word of God.

Challenges from Papyrology

Papyrology, the study of ancient papyrus manuscripts, plays a crucial role in textual criticism. The dating of these manuscripts is vital for understanding the history of the biblical text. However, there has been a trend among some papyrologists to redate early New Testament papyri to later periods, which can affect our understanding of the transmission and reliability of the New Testament.

The Importance of Early Papyri

Early New Testament papyri, such as P52 (the Rylands Library Papyrus), are critical for establishing the early existence and widespread use of the New Testament texts. These papyri provide evidence that the New Testament was written and circulated within the first century, close to the time of the events they describe.

Redating Efforts and Their Implications

Efforts to redate these early papyri to later periods can cast doubt on the early authorship and dissemination of the New Testament. However, conservative scholars argue for the traditional dating based on paleographic and historical evidence. The early dating of these papyri supports the reliability and authenticity of the New Testament documents.

Defending the Bible Against Modern Challenges

In the face of these various challenges, conservative evangelical Christian apologists have tirelessly defended the integrity and authority of the Bible. Their work is crucial for upholding the truth of God's Word in an age of skepticism and disbelief.

Affirming Biblical Inerrancy

The doctrine of biblical inerrancy asserts that the Scriptures, in their original autographs, are without error. This belief is based on the nature of God as truthful and incapable of deceit. Numbers 23:19 states, "God is not a man, that He should lie, nor a son of man, that He should repent; Has He said, and will He not do it? Or has He spoken, and will He not make it good?" Upholding biblical inerrancy is essential for maintaining the trustworthiness of Scripture.

Combating Theological Liberalism

Theological liberalism often seeks to reinterpret or dismiss biblical teachings to align with contemporary cultural values. Conservative apologists counter these efforts by affirming the timeless truth of the Bible. Jude 1:3 exhorts believers to "contend earnestly for the faith which was once for all handed down to the saints." This call to defend the faith involves standing firm on the clear teachings of Scripture, regardless of cultural trends.

Engaging in Scholarly Debate

Conservative scholars engage in rigorous scholarly debate, providing evidence and arguments for the reliability and authenticity of the Bible. This includes addressing higher criticism, defending traditional authorship and dating, and upholding the importance of literal translation and accurate textual criticism. 1 Peter 3:15 encourages believers to "always be ready to make a defense to everyone who asks you to give an account for the hope that is in you, yet with gentleness and reverence."

The Role of Faith and Reason

While intellectual defense of the Bible is crucial, faith also plays a vital role in accepting its truths. Hebrews 11:1 defines faith as "the assurance of things hoped for, the conviction of things not seen." Faith and reason work together, as reason supports the credibility of the Bible, and faith embraces its divine revelation.

Trusting in God's Word

Believers are called to trust in the Word of God, recognizing its divine origin and authority. Psalm 119:160 declares, "The sum of Your word is truth, and every one of Your righteous ordinances is everlasting." This trust is based on the character of God and the consistency of His revelation throughout history.

Living Out Biblical Truths

The ultimate goal of defending the Bible is to live out its truths in daily life. James 1:22-25 urges believers to be "doers of the word, and not merely hearers who delude themselves." The transformative power of the Scriptures is evident in the lives of those who faithfully follow its teachings.

Conclusion

The battle for the Bible is an ongoing struggle to maintain the integrity and authority of God's Word in the face of numerous challenges. Conservative evangelical Christian apologists play a crucial role in this battle, defending the Bible against false dichotomies, higher criticism, textual skepticism, and cultural relativism. By affirming biblical inerrancy, engaging in scholarly debate, and trusting in the divine revelation of Scripture, believers can stand firm in their faith and proclaim the truth of God's Word to a skeptical world.

www.ingramcontent.com/pod-product-compliance
Lightning Source LLC
LaVergne TN
LVHW041334080426
835512LV00006B/446